THE UPPER ROOM

WHERE THE WORLD MEETS TO PRAY

Sarah Wilke
Publisher

INTERDENOMINATIONAL
INTERNATIONAL
INTERRACIAL

33 LANGUAGES
Multiple formats are available in some languages

The Upper Room
January–April 2015
Edited by Susan Hibbins

The Upper Room © BRF 2015
The Bible Reading Fellowship
15 The Chambers, Vineyard, Abingdon OX14 3FE
Tel: 01865 319700; Fax: 01865 319701
Email: enquiries@brf.org.uk
Website: www.brf.org.uk
BRF is a Registered Charity

ISBN 978 0 85746 126 1

Acknowledgments
The New Revised Standard Version of the Bible, Anglicised Edition, copyright
© 1989, 1995 by the Division of Christian Education of the National Council
of the Churches of Christ in the USA. Used by permission. All rights reserved.

The Holy Bible, New International Version, copyright © 1979, 1984, 2011 by
Biblica. Used by permission of Hodder & Stoughton Publishers, an Hachette
UK company. All rights reserved. 'NIV' is a registered trademark of Biblica. UK
trademark number 1448790.

Extracts from the Authorised Version of the Bible (The King James Bible),
the rights in which are vested in the Crown, are reproduced by permission of
the Crown's Patentee, Cambridge University Press.

Extracts from CEB copyright © 2011 by Common English Bible.

Printed by Gutenberg Press, Tarxien, Malta

The Upper Room: how to use this book

The Upper Room is ideal in helping us spend a quiet time with God each day. Each daily entry is based on a passage of scripture, and is followed by a meditation and prayer. Each person who contributes a meditation to the magazine seeks to relate their experience of God in a way that will help those who use The Upper Room every day.

Here are some guidelines to help you make best use of The Upper Room:

1. Read the passage of Scripture. It is a good idea to read it more than once, in order to have a fuller understanding of what it is about and what you can learn from it.
2. Read the meditation. How does it relate to your own experience? Can you identify with what the writer has outlined from their own experience or understanding?
3. Pray the written prayer. Think about how you can use it to relate to people you know, or situations that need your prayers today.
4. Think about the contributor who has written the meditation. Some Upper Room users include this person in their prayers for the day.
5. Meditate on the 'Thought for the Day', the 'Link2Life' and the 'Prayer Focus', perhaps using them again as the focus for prayer or direction for action.

Why is it important to have a daily quiet time? Many people will agree that it is the best way of keeping in touch every day with the God who sustains us, and who sends us out to do his will and show his love to the people we encounter each day. Meeting with God in this way reassures us of his presence with us, helps us to discern his will for us and makes us part of his worldwide family of Christian people through our prayers.

I hope that you will be encouraged as you use the magazine regularly as part of your daily devotions, and that God will richly bless you as you read his word and seek to learn more about him.

Susan Hibbins
UK Editor

In Times of/For Help with . . .

Below is a list of entries in this copy of *The Upper Room* relating to situations or emotions with which we may need help:

Addiction: Jan 20; Feb 27

Anger: Jan 14; Apr 28

Anxiety: Feb 14, 26, 28; Mar 15; Apr 7

Assurance: Jan 25; Mar 1; Apr 13

Bible reading: Jan 7, 12; Feb 3; 20; Mar 14, 27

Celebration: Jan 19; Mar 2; Apr 3

Change: Jan 22; Feb 28; Mar 31; Apr 30

Christian community: Jan 18; Feb. 1, 16; Mar 28; Apr. 10

Compassion: Jan 9, 14; Feb 23; Mar 5, 11; Apr 12, 20

Creation/nature's beauty: Jan 15, 31; Feb 5, 13

Death/grief: Jan 20, 28; Feb 9, 11; Apr 5

Doubt: Jan 5, 8, 21; Feb 4; Apr 4

Encouragement: Jan 1 29; Apr 9

Evangelism: Jan 21; Feb 10

Family: Jan 9, 28; Feb 1, 19; Mar 14, 24; Apr 9, 21

Fear: Jan 3, 11; Apr 17, 27, 30

Forgiveness: Feb 13, 23; Mar 17; Apr 15, 28

Friendship: Jan 29; Feb 13; Apr 8

Freedom: Jan 11, 20; Mar 27

Generosity/giving: Mar 23; Apr 14

God's goodness/love: Jan 9, 25; Feb 1, 27; Mar 12, 31; Apr 9, 18

God's presence: Jan 3, 30; Feb 2, 22, 28; Mar 15; Apr 26, 27

God's provision: Jan 1, 5; Feb 11; Mar 1, 7; Apr 7

Gratitude: Jan 16; Mar 5, 27, 30

Growth: Jan 22, 31; Feb 15, 21; Apr 30

Guidance: Jan 30; Mar 29; Apr 26

Healing/Illness: Jan 3, 26; Feb 2, 19; Mar 3, 19; Apr 1, 3, 30

Hope: Mar 24; Apr 4, 15

Hospitality: Jan 13; Mar 16; Apr 19

Job issues: Jan 18, 27; Feb 26

Judging: Jan 14, 24; Mar 16; Apr 14, 16

Lent/Easter: Mar 4, 8, 22, 28; Apr 1, 3, 4, 5

Living our faith: Jan 6, 18; Feb 3, 18, 25; Mar 2, 21; Apr 19, 25

Loneliness: Jan 15

Loss: Jan 28

Mission/outreach: Jan 12, 24; Feb 12, 27; Apr 11, 21

New beginnings: Jan 11; Feb 21; 26; Mar 8, 18; Apr 5

Obedience: Feb 24; Mar 9, 19

Parenting: Jan 6, 13; Feb 17; Mar 13, 14

Patience: Mar 31; Apr 2, 24

Peace/Unrest: Mar 17

Prayer: Jan 2, 27; Feb 4, 8, 24; Mar 3, 25; Apr 16, 28

Renewal: Jan 26, 31; Feb 15; Apr 22

Salvation: Jan 16; Feb 10, 21; Mar 26; Apr 18

Serving: Jan 1; Feb 12; Mar 3, 5; Apr 2

Sin: Jan. 25; Feb 12

Speaking about faith: Jan 4, 21; Mar 13, 28; Apr 29

Social issues: Feb 2, 9 18; Mar 20

Spiritual gifts: Jan 8, 10; Apr 23

Spiritual practices: Jan 7, 26; Feb. 3, 8; 25; Mar 4, 23, 30; Apr 6, 22

Stress: Jan 27; Feb 6 16; Mar 12

Tragedy: Feb 7, 9, 16; Apr 20

Transitions: Apr 15, 27

Trust: Jan 2, 27; Feb. 6, 14, 26; Mar 7, 10; Apr 17, 24

Weakness: Mar 21, 22

Worry: Jan 23, 30; Feb 5; Mar 10, 25; Apr 1, 6

The Courage to Ask

'Do not worry about anything, but in everything by prayer and supplication with thanksgiving let your requests be made known to God. And the peace of God, which surpasses all understanding, will guard your hearts and your minds in Christ Jesus' (Philippians 4:6–7).

When I preached that day in the Mexico City church, my sermon topic was about my own struggles with forgiveness. After the service, a young mother approached me with her son. Something in my words, she said, had touched the ten-year-old boy, who had been trying to forgive his father for abandoning the family a few years before.

The woman and I spoke for a precious few moments before I had to turn to greet other worshippers who had gathered around. Soon I felt a tug at my sleeve. I looked down to see the shy and pleading face of the boy.

'Will you pray for me?'

It's a question I've heard often since coming to work for this prayer ministry. Yes, maybe it just goes with the territory. But surely all of us hunger for another's prayer, whether or not we are able to put the question on our lips. The power of prayer comes in relationship with God—and with one another.

Some people may find it easy to answer yes to the request and make a mental note to add a name to their prayer list. But for me, the more I've heard the question, the more I can't help but hear the sense of immediacy and the heaviness of a heart. If you have the courage to ask for another's prayer, I've come to believe, you probably need it at that very moment.

And so I took the boy's hand and we knelt together at the altar. I don't remember my exact words, but I know God does, as he remembers everyone who lets their 'requests be made known to God'.

Sarah Wilke
Publisher

My name is Dory Restrepo Sánchez. I am a pastor with the Colombia Methodist Church serving in a rural community near Cali. Two years ago I assumed the duties of distributor for El *Aposento Alto* in Colombia, Venezuela, and Ecuador.

Bishop Isaías Gutiérrez, former editor of El *Aposento Alto* for all of South America, travelled to Colombia in the early 1990s and joined with the Methodist Church of Colombia to begin publishing the magazine. In 1998 the circulation of the magazine was small, a mere 20 copies. By the end of 1998, Reverend Juan Guerrero and his wife, Alexandra, were named as official distributors. The circulation of El *Aposento Alto* in Colombia, Venezuela and Ecuador now totals 10,000 copies.

It is a privilege to be a member of the El *Aposento Alto* family and to offer the good news of the gospel to many people by means of this small but important resource.

Pastor Dory Restrepo Sánchez
Distributor for Colombia, Venezuela and Ecuador

The Editor writes...

Last year I decided to do what I'm sure many of you have done already: to read the Bible in a year. When I looked at a suggested schedule that would ensure I completed Genesis to Revelation in the time, however, I found that, in order to pay enough attention to what I was reading, it would take me far longer than a year. I find it is best to read slowly and with the help of a commentary, so that I can understand fully what I am reading. So I have given up on the schedule and am taking it at my own pace.

Two phrases stood out for me almost straight away in the early chapters of Genesis. However you regard the creation stories and the story of Noah, there are little illuminations stored away in them which show us immediately what God is like. The first was in Genesis 3:9, where God is walking in the garden in the evening, looking for Adam. 'Where are you?' asks God. The second is in chapter 5:6, where God is sorry that he made humankind, since they have messed up spectacularly with what he has given them, and 'it grieved him to his heart'.

To me, this set the tone for all that is to follow in the Bible: firstly, God never ceases to seek for us. He wants to spend time with us because he cares for us and about us. Often people ask how they can find God, but it is the other way round: God is seeking for them. Secondly, God is grieved by our sin. He has given us so much and when we misuse it and mistreat each other, it grieves him—and yet, he forgives us. All the books in the Bible tell us of God's dealing with the world: of his seeking for us, forgiving us and above all loving us so much that he sent his Son to show us once and for all what God is like. Quite a story!

Susan Hibbins
Editor of the UK edition

No Small Efforts

Read John 6:8–13

The Lord will fulfil his purpose for me; your steadfast love, O Lord, endures forever.

Psalm 138:8 (NRSV)

Often I fall into the trap of comparing myself to other people. I look at the impact they seem to have on the world and feel as if I don't measure up. One day, when I was feeling inferior, God gave me a new perspective on the familiar loaves-and-fishes story. Instead of focusing on the miracle itself or on the boy who offered up his lunch, I thought about the woman who might have made the lunch. I imagined her kneading the dough with work-worn hands, carefully wrapping the fresh loaves and fish in a cloth, and handing the bundle to the boy with a kiss on his cheek. To her, these must have seemed such small, ordinary tasks. How could she have anticipated that the meal she had packed for her son that day would have such eternal significance?

That reminded me of the many ways that God takes our small efforts and uses them to feed people physically, emotionally and spiritually. So when I feel that I should be doing bigger things with my life, I remind myself of the loaves and fishes. My job is to do the tasks in front of me. God's job—God's delight—is to use them to feed the world.

Prayer: *Dear Lord, help us to trust you to use us for your purpose. Amen*

Thought for the day: What small task can I offer to God today?

Sara Matson (Minnesota, US)

Speechless

Read Philippians 4:4–7

The Spirit helps us in our weakness; for we do not know how to pray as we ought, but that very Spirit intercedes with sighs too deep for words.
Romans 8:26 (NRSV)

In this age of communication—tweets, texts, webcams, blogs and status updates—we are rarely speechless. But coming to God during the most difficult times, during the most daunting situations, often leaves us speechless. We are utterly at a loss for what to say, what to pray, or what to ask. How do we bring to God our deepest concerns when we cannot find the words?

When we communicate with people it is important to be clear and concise. But God has no such expectations. He knows that sometimes our circumstances leave us totally speechless, and long ago he gave us the Holy Spirit to intervene for us in just those situations.

Prayer: *Dear God, thank you for understanding our silence, our quiet moments and our tears. Thank you, God, for knowing what we need before we ask. As Jesus taught us, we pray, 'Our Father which art in heaven, Hallowed be thy name. Thy kingdom come. Thy will be done in earth, as it is in heaven. Give us this day our daily bread. And forgive us our debts, as we forgive our debtors. And lead us not into temptation, but deliver us from evil: For thine is the kingdom, and the power, and the glory, for ever.'* Amen*

Thought for the day: Through the Holy Spirit, God knows all our prayers.

Latoya M. Morris (Virginia, US)

* Matthew 6:9–13 (KJV)

Choose to Trust

Read Psalm 23:1–6

Even though I walk through the darkest valley, I will fear no evil, for you are with me.
Psalm 23:4 (NIV)

A relatively routine surgery developed life-threatening complications, and my husband's life was now hanging by a thread. This unexpected situation brought me face to face with the reality that I was not in control of my life. But I knew God was present.

Obviously, I had not chosen these circumstances, but I knew I could choose how I would respond to them. Sitting in that ICU room, I reflected on the fact that when I accepted Jesus Christ as my personal Saviour, he became my divine shepherd. Meditating on the unlimited, timeless, supreme power of my shepherd filled my heart with comfort and peace. I chose at that moment to trust my shepherd—just as King David describes in Psalm 23.

Sudden, unexpected turns in life and anticipating an uncertain future can cripple us with doubt and fear. These situations steal our peace and stifle our joy. However, we have an antidote. Peace and comfort—even joy—will return when we remember that we are the sheep of God's pasture. Let us choose to trust our Great Shepherd's divine care and wisdom.

Prayer: *Thank you, Great Shepherd, for leading us in paths that are best for our spiritual growth. You provide all we need, and we praise you for your loving, faithful care. Amen*

Thought for the day: We can rest in peace, knowing we are in the care of a loving God.

Sandra Hastings (Germany)

Perfect in Weakness

Read 2 Corinthians 12:6–10

The Lord said to Paul, 'My power is made perfect in weakness.'
2 Corinthians 12:9 (NIV)

Mabel was known as a prayer warrior. She was always willing to intercede with God on behalf of others. This was one of her gifts. Being available to others was another. In her later years she had become discouraged when her poor eyesight had become an obstacle in her desire to serve. Once, she had tried to call a friend, misread the number and dialled incorrectly. Typical of Mabel, she began asking the person at the other end of the phone if he was a person of faith and about his life. She had a long conversation with 'Wrong Number' and gave him a lot of encouragement, which she said seemed to change his tone and attitude as they talked. He thanked her for the call. She realised, then, that God could use even her poor eyesight as an avenue for service.

Mabel's example is a reminder to me that God can use not only our gifts and graces but also our weaknesses and 'wrong numbers'. More and more I'm discovering that God is in the detours of our lives. Indeed, those detours often become thoroughfares through which we experience epiphany.

Prayer: *Dear God, show us ways every day that we can be available to serve those around us. Amen*

Thought for the day: God can turn our 'wrong numbers' into opportunities.

Davis Chappell (Tennessee, US)

Human Frailty

Read Luke 7:18–23

Jesus answering said unto [John's disciples], Go your way, and tell John what things ye have seen and heard; how that the blind see, the lame walk, the lepers are cleansed, the deaf hear, the dead are raised, to the poor the gospel is preached.

Luke 7:22 (KJV)

After John the Baptist had had the privilege of baptising Jesus, he also witnessed the Spirit descending from heaven as a dove and lighting on Jesus. John heard God's voice announcing from heaven, 'You are my Son, the Beloved; with you I am well pleased' (Luke 3:22, NRSV). Yet only a short time later, John was confused enough about Jesus that he sent two of his disciples to ask him, 'Are you the one who is to come, or are we to wait for another?' (Luke 7:19, NRSV).

In spite of John's display of doubt, Jesus went on to proclaim John the greatest of all the prophets. I believe that God's gospel includes this story to reassure us when our faith wavers. It is human nature to be plagued by uncertainties. God gave us inquisitive minds and expects us to ask difficult but honest questions when we encounter matters that affect our faith. Perhaps Jesus knew that believers would need to have their faith bolstered from time to time so he asked God to send the Holy Spirit to live inside us for ever and be our comforter (see John 14:16–18).

Prayer: *Dear Lord, thank you for understanding when we doubt. Strengthen our faith when we struggle. Amen*

Thought for the day: In times of doubt, I can lean on God's word and the Holy Spirit to renew my faith.

Carol P. Nyborg (North Carolina, US)

Imitation

Read Ephesians 4:30—5:2

Be imitators of God, as beloved children, and live in love, as Christ loved us and gave himself up for us, a fragrant offering and sacrifice to God.
Ephesians 5:1–2 (NRSV)

Our two-year-old son, Caleb, loves to imitate us. He likes to try on our slippers and shoes and clomp around in them. He wants to vacuum or shovel snow when one of his parents is doing the task. He often repeats our sentences, mimicking the intonation exactly.

Caleb's longing to be just like his parents is a universal desire of children. And child-development experts suggest that such imitated actions present powerful lessons to a young child, leaving lasting impressions on the developing mind.

Our son's imitation helps us understand Paul's instruction in Ephesians 5:1. Because God is our heavenly Father, it is natural and right to imitate him. Through such imitation we learn how to live most fully.

We learn how to love others by trying to love them as God does. We learn compassion, generosity and forgiveness by practising them in our daily lives. The more we imitate God, the easier and more natural it becomes. Through imitation, we become known as God's children.

Prayer: *Heavenly Father, fill us with the childlike desire to be just like you. Draw us closer to you, and fill us with your love for those around us. Amen*

Thought for the day: How well do I imitate God in word and deed?

Anita Dualeh (Minnesota, US)

Physical and Spiritual Nourishment

Read Psalm 119:1–16

How sweet are your words to my taste, sweeter than honey to my mouth!
Psalm 119:103 (NRSV)

A few years ago I decided that I was overweight, so I began a diet and exercise regime. I had to control the portions and the types of food I consumed. I needed to reduce the cakes, chocolates and sweets and eat more salads, fruit and other nourishing foods.

One day my wife gave me some nuts for a snack. I never liked to eat nuts in the past, but I took a handful and ate them. I found that I quite liked them! My sense of taste had changed over the years. I discovered that the fruit and salads I once avoided are now pleasing and tasty to me. I no longer crave snacks such as chocolates and other sweets.

Psalm 119 reminds us that we should long for God's word. Just as we digest our food, so we should consume God's words. The food we eat provides us with energy, strength and life. Consequently, when we read, study and absorb what we read in the Bible, we can grow as Christians every day.

I now try to control what I eat by choosing more wholesome, nutritious foods rather than rich, fatty sweets and desserts. Likewise, we should look at what we digest spiritually. Just as we have to make time to eat properly, so we should make time to digest what God says to us when we read the Bible and pray.

Prayer: *Dear Father, thank you for your holy word, the Bible. Help us to digest your word and use it as our spiritual source of energy day by day. Amen*

Thought for the day: Spending time with God daily makes a good spiritual diet.

Mark Wallace (Suffolk, England)

Pursuing in God's Strength

Read Judges 6:11–27
When the angel of the Lord appeared to Gideon, he said, 'The Lord is with you, mighty warrior.'
Judges 6:12 (NIV)

Years ago, I felt God's call to work as a children's minister in a large church. But all I could see were my inadequacies for such a task. After resisting the call and asking God for a sign, I soon discovered that as I yielded to and depended on the Lord, I was given the ability.

In myself, I am inadequate, but I trust that God will not lead me to complete a task without also giving me the ability to accomplish it. With this in mind, I followed God's call and served in children's ministry for 13 years. Seeing the lives of children changed was rewarding. To this day, I periodically hear from some of them—requesting prayers or financial support as they serve as missionaries, pastors or even children's ministers.

I see similarities between my experience and the story of Gideon. God called Gideon a 'mighty warrior' long before Gideon saw himself capable of carrying out the task God required of him.

I want to be like Gideon, trusting that no task is too great because our God equips us to accomplish the tasks we are called to do.

Prayer: *Dear God, help us to follow your leading and to trust that you will give us what we need for the tasks you call us to do. Amen*

Thought for the day: When God calls us to a task, he equips us to accomplish it.

Rebecca Seaton (Tennessee, US)

Abandoned but Not Hopeless

Read 2 Corinthians 4:6–15

The Lord watches over the foreigner and sustains the fatherless and the widow.

Psalm 146:9 (NIV)

'What can I do? My father left us at the beginning of the year. We have not seen or heard from him since!' Mandy is only eleven and these words from her letter touched me deeply. My own father was not absent, but he was emotionally distant. He was a good provider, but wartime experiences and his own troubled childhood made him withdrawn in his relationships with his children. Although we always knew he loved us, this did not stop me from asking the same question Mandy asked, 'What can I do?'

Talking with Mandy seemed to help her. I encouraged her to focus on the lives of those around her. She began to shower love on her mother and her young brothers and sisters. Then, when the time was right, we spoke about God's love, a Father's love that never fails.

I don't know what the future holds for Mandy. I only know that listening to her helped. Gentle direction helped. Leading her to focus on God's love helped. I believe God is moving in her life. She is less stressed, and she prays for her family and her dad. She tells me that she now feels she is indeed doing something!

Prayer: *Dear Father God, open our ears and hearts to know the hurts of others. Give us wisdom to speak and act in helpful ways. In Jesus' name. Amen*

Thought for the day: Focusing on God's love can bring comfort and hope to me and to others.

Faye Roots (Queensland, Australia)

Pictures of God

Read 1 Peter 4:10–11

Each of you should use whatever gift you have received to serve others, as faithful stewards of God's grace in its various forms.
1 Peter 4:10 (NIV)

My wife belongs to an art group that meets once a week to create pictures, usually in watercolour. All the artists are very talented; yet each has a different style. Once, my wife showed me a group of works all based on the same photograph of a house and property. I couldn't believe it. The pictures were so different, yet I could see the similarity by looking at the photograph. The artists had all viewed the same picture but used their talents and creativity to create beautiful but different paintings.

I see a lesson in the work of these artists. We all have been given circumstances in our lives, and God wants us to use our talents and creativity to create a beautiful environment around us. Sometimes our circumstances are commonplace or dull, and sometimes they are ugly or threatening. Sometimes we think they are so wonderful that we don't know how to improve on them. But God wants us to put our own touch on them, to fill them with our love and make them beautiful for others to see. As a result, people will know that he is working through us. That's one of the ways people get to know God—by seeing him working in us and through us.

Prayer: *Generous God, guide us to use our talents to be a picture of your love for other people. Amen*

Thought for the day: What picture of God does my life display today?

Gary Hubley (Maine, US)

Still Constrained?

Read 2 Corinthians 10:1–5

Stand firm… and do not let yourselves be burdened again by a yoke of slavery.
Galatians 5:1 (NIV)

For years, whenever my dog and I walked through our garden on the way to the gate, we had to manoeuvre around a trampoline. Finally, the children grown, my husband and I decided we could get rid of it. I relished the thought of not having to encounter it and I expected that the dog would be just as happy, since his lead regularly got tangled in the trampoline legs. Surprisingly, the first time we walked through the garden after the trampoline was down, instead of traipsing through the new wide-open space, he clung tightly to the old path and I followed. The old obstruction was gone, but we acted as if it were still there.

This experience reminded me of what can happen when we become believers. When we accept Christ, we are made new and sin has no power over us. So I wondered why I still struggle with fear. I realised that the same force that kept the family dog and me on the worn path keeps me struggling: familiarity. The dog and I continued to choose the comfortable and safe path, one that didn't require much discernment. In a similar way, even when we have received Christ, we may plod along the path of old thought patterns—but we do have a new power over them. We can consciously choose to dismiss old thought patterns that don't produce fruit and walk the path of freedom.

Prayer: *Heavenly Father, help us to examine each thought so that all our thoughts may glorify you. Amen*

Thought for the day: 'We take captive every thought to make it obedient to Christ' (2 Corinthians 10:5).

Debbie Middlebrook (Georgia, US)

Crows and Nightingales

Read Job 32:6–9

'Age should speak; advanced years should teach wisdom.'
Job 32:6–9 (NIV)

Members of our church hold regular services at local retirement homes. Fresh filtered coffee fragranced the room as our time of sharing one day drew to a close. Over refreshments we chatted to the residents.

'Well, everyone was in good voice today,' I said to one elderly lady. She nodded. Then, with a wink, she added, 'Yes! I could hear you croaking—just like me!'

For a moment words failed me. I thought I had been in good voice that day. However, her words of consolation made me smile: 'Never mind; God makes crows as well as nightingales.' We laughed together at the end of a perfect time of worship.

The Lord teaches us in many ways. His sense of humour and timing are perfect. The quality of our worship is more important than the tunefulness of our singing. It's true that 'crows' may not sing as beautifully as nightingales, but the praises of both make sweet music in his ears.

Prayer: *Help us, O Lord, to praise and worship you with all our hearts. Amen*

Thought for the day: Our worship is sweet music to God.

Pauline Pullan (Yorkshire, England)

Let the Little Children Come

Read Mark 10:13–16

Jesus said to [the chief priests and the scribes], 'Yes; have you never read, "Out of the mouths of infants and nursing babies you have prepared praise for yourself?"'
Matthew 21:16 (NRSV)

One night as we were going to sleep, I heard my young grandson singing, in his two-year-old way, one of the most difficult church hymns. Just by being present in church, he had learned this hymn and made it part of his life.

Young children often get restless during worship. When this happens with my grandchildren, I usually take them out of the service. I worry about their disturbing others. But Jesus said to let the little children come to him and not to stop them (Mark 10:14, 15). These words convince me that welcoming children to worship and into the family of the church is more important than hurrying them out when they squirm or make a little noise.

I know that in the world outside the church, my grandchildren will encounter many distractions that will draw their attention away from God. That's why I feel that bringing them to God through the worship and fellowship of the church is an essential responsibility.

Prayer: *Dear God, help us to remember and take seriously our responsibility to help the children in our lives grow up knowing you and your Son, Jesus. Amen*

Thought for the day: How does my church welcome and nurture its children?

Elenka Angelova (Ruse, Bulgaria)

PRAYER FOCUS: FOR OUR CHILDREN WHO ARE FAR FROM THE CHURCH

Bless, Not Curse

Read Luke 6:27–38

Bless those who persecute you; bless and do not curse them.
Romans 12:14 (NRSV)

Sometimes it seems as if every day we encounter a difficult person—whether a colleague, a neighbour or a family member. We may try to avoid them, complain about them or even confront the one who offends us. We may spend a tremendous amount of time allowing our conflict with this person to rob us of our joy and energy.

Jesus said, 'In this world you will have trouble. But take heart! I have overcome the world' (John 16:33, NIV). In Christ we have peace. When faced with a difficult person we can remember that we are not to 'imitate what is evil but what is good' (3 John 1:11, NIV).

As difficult as it may seem, we are to speak blessings on the other person—for God blesses those who bless others. Instead of focusing on someone's negative attributes, we can find at least one trait that we admire or respect about the person. Maybe they're a hard worker or a talented musician or a caring grandparent. Instead of gossiping about other people or arguing with them, we can pray for them. We cloud God's light when we allow anger or insensitivity to control us. Once we start focusing on the positive and turn to God in prayer, his love can shine through us.

Prayer: *Dear Lord, help us to speak blessings on those we find difficult to love. Teach us to pray for them. In Jesus' name we pray. Amen*

Thought for the day: Today I will look for the image of God in everyone I meet.

Danielle J. Lang (Maryland, US)

Not Just Specks

Read Psalm 8:3–9

When I look at your heavens, the work of your fingers, the moon and the stars that you have established; what are human beings that you are mindful of them, mortals that you care for them?
Psalm 8:3–4 (NRSV)

As a young boy I would sometimes lie outside on a blanket at night, looking at the stars. I used to think I could count all of them, but I learned in time about the true vastness of the universe. The whole human race is but a tiny speck on the earth. Our earth is just a dot in the Milky Way system with its millions of heavenly bodies, and the Milky Way system is only a small cluster of heavenly bodies in the limitless expanse of the universe. How easy it is to feel alone in all that space!

Our God who created this great universe can see from one of its 'ends' to the other. Although we may sometimes feel very insignificant, we know that we are significant because God created us and knows everything about each of us—our needs and concerns, our hopes and dreams and our fears. He stands ready to comfort, to calm and to bring us joy and peace. To him we are not specks far off somewhere in space. To him, we are known and precious and loved.

I still look up to the heavens on dark clear nights and enjoy the beauty of the stars, convinced that God knows exactly where I am and loves me mightily. He loves each one of us.

Prayer: *Dear God, we praise you for your power and majesty and also for your love and concern for each of us. Amen*

Thought for the day: We are not just specks in the world but are wonderfully created by a loving God.

Malcolm Dirksen (South Dakota, US)

PRAYER FOCUS: THOSE WHO FEEL ALONE

Living Thanks

Read Luke 17:11–19
One of [the lepers], when he saw he was healed, came back, praising God in a loud voice.
Luke 17:15 (NIV)

Whenever I hear the story of the ten lepers, I am amazed that only one came back to thank Jesus. After all, Jesus had given them their lives back. They had been encumbered by a horrible skin disease, which left them outcasts. Jesus' response allowed them to be reunited with their families and to be part of their community again. Jesus gave them life. What a gift! But only one returned to say thank you.

I can easily point a finger at the lepers who didn't return; I can ask, 'How could they be so ungrateful?' Yet, reflecting on my own life, I know I must appear as the nine, so intent on the false importance of my busyness that I forget to give thanks to God. I too have been delivered from a horrible disease: sin. It would have left me an outcast just like those lepers—doomed to die alone—were it not for my Lord and Saviour Jesus Christ. Salvation is worthy of my continuous thanks and gratitude, but God goes further and heaps blessing upon blessing on us. I have resolved to give thanks, not only in my prayers of gratitude but also in the way I live. Living with thankful spirits helps us better to witness to what God has done for us.

Prayer: *Dear Lord Jesus, thank you for delivering us and for giving us life. Help us to live each day with thankful hearts and grateful spirits so that we may witness to your amazing grace. Amen*

Thought for the day: We show our thanks to God by the way we live.

Gina Bylsma (California, US)

Threads of Love

Read Psalm 121:1–8

Jesus came and stood among [the disciples] and said, 'Peace be with you.' After he said this, he showed them his hands and his side.
John 20:19–20 (NRSV)

I love to knit. So when my dear friend was battling cancer, I made her a shawl. At first, I just concentrated on the pattern, making sure to get the number of stitches right and keeping the rows even. Then, as I settled into the rhythm of knitting, I began to pray. I prayed for my friend's comfort. I prayed that Christ would hold her in his arms. I felt my prayer become tangible as the shawl grew longer.

One of the last times I saw my friend, she was resting on her sofa, covered by the shawl I had made for her. And while I knew that there was no earthly cure for her illness, I also felt some measure of peace. Something as commonplace as yarn had been threaded through with compassion. Christ was there for both of us. I think that is what peace is: filling the darkness of pain and grief with love.

Prayer: *Dear Lord, we ask that you use our hands and our hearts to bring your peace to those who need comfort as we pray, 'Our Father which art in heaven, Hallowed be thy name. Thy kingdom come. Thy will be done, as in heaven, so in earth. Give us day by day our daily bread. And forgive us our sins; for we also forgive every one that is indebted to us. And lead us not into temptation; but deliver us from evil.'* Amen*

Thought for the day: Christ's love can flow through the works of our hands.

Patricia Marks (Georgia, US)

PRAYER FOCUS: THOSE FACING A FRIEND'S DEATH
* Luke 11:2–4 (KJV)

For the Good of All

Read Galatians 6:7–10

Whenever we have an opportunity, let us work for the good of all.
Galatians 6:10 (NRSV)

On a recent flight, I read in the airline company's in-flight magazine that the year before they had received 114,845 CVs, but hired
only 2499 people. I was then impressed by what I learned about
the way they treat their employees once they are hired. They don't
focus intensely on rules or policy applications (except those related
to safety). Instead, they give their employees freedom to be themselves, to do what they discern to be right in taking care of their
customers. They have one overriding rule, the Golden Rule—treat-
ing others as you want to be treated. They hire people with passionate servant hearts and empower them to do what's right. They
have found that—when treated in this way—their employees consistently surprise, delight and amaze their customers.

I began to compare this company's policy to our opportunity as
Christians. As set forth by God, we—the Church—will be truly committed to Jesus Christ, enjoying our freedom in Christ, living by the
Golden Rule, having passionate servant hearts, and empowered to
use our God-given gifts and talents in doing what is right. Such a
Body will also consistently serve those around it. A congregation
whose members walk as Jesus walked and focus on people will also
surprise, delight and amaze their community. Those around us will
see us showing loving and deliberate acts of kindness every day.
Isn't this a picture of God's way for the family of Christ?

Prayer: *Dear God, fill us with zeal to be your people in everything we do.
Help us to focus on serving you and serving those around us. Amen*

Thought for the day: God empowers us to serve excellently.

Andy Baker (Tennessee, US)

PRAYER FOCUS: AIRLINE EMPLOYEES

Do You Remember When?

Read Psalm 107:1–9

Take care and watch yourselves closely, so as neither to forget the things that your eyes have seen nor to let them slip from your mind all the days of your life.

Deuteronomy 4:9 (NRSV)

'Remember when…?' That's the question we asked our niece at her 21st birthday party as we launched into a list of 21 things we remembered most about her: her first attempt to bake a cake, her first date, moving away for college, among other events. At the end of our list family and friends laughed at the funny memories. 'I can't believe you remembered all that stuff!' she said as she hugged and thanked us.

I realise that lists are tools we use to document important facts or events. To-do lists remind us of things we need to accomplish; shopping lists keep us on track when we shop; keeping a list of upcoming bills helps us stay within our budget.

Lists can help strengthen our faith. Writing down the many ways that God has touched our lives, looking back over prayer lists and journal entries of answered prayers, and recording Bible verses that we're meditating on can enrich our spiritual lives. These activities can help us 'remember when' God's presence was especially meaningful for us.

Prayer: *Dear Father, thank you for your steadfast presence. Help us to tell others about your marvellous works. Amen*

Thought for the day: Remembering God's past faithfulness helps us trust him with the future.

Dorothea M. Love (California, US)

From Bondage to Joy

Read Romans 8:28–31

Those who go out weeping, carrying seed to sow, will return with songs of joy, carrying sheaves with them.

Psalm 126:6 (NIV)

Michael grew up in a close, loving family; yet, in high school he began using drugs. After struggling for some time with addiction, he had recently completed rehabilitation and seemed to be on the right track. Then Michael showed signs of a relapse. One afternoon, he went downstairs and turned on his music. Michael was later found dead; he was 23. Those who knew him were heartbroken by this senseless loss.

The service celebrating Michael's life was packed. Many of those attending were young people who were with him during his last rehab; they had believed his would be a success story. At the grave-side service, I spoke with a mother whose son was still struggling with addiction; her son was devastated by Michael's death. He expressed it this way: 'Only with God's help can I ever be free from this!'

With this in mind, we turn to scripture for comfort. Psalm 126:6 reminds us that in times of grief, God will provide us with strength, joy, and healing—allowing us to bear fruit for his kingdom.

Prayer: *Dear Lord, help us to pray believing that, even through tears and broken hearts, all things come together for good for those who seek you. Amen*

Thought for the day: Only God can give us an abundant life.

Dan Nelson (North Carolina, US)

Courage to Witness

Read Acts 5:27–32

Let the redeemed of the Lord tell their story.
Psalm 107:2 (NIV)

While in the hospital for three weeks with pregnancy complications, I spent time reading my Bible and *The Upper Room*. Also, one of the nurses brought me a radio that I tuned to my favourite Christian music station. The music was soothing and peaceful.

However, as much as I loved listening to this music, a part of me wanted to turn it off whenever someone walked in the room. I don't know if I was ashamed or just didn't want to make anyone feel uncomfortable. Regardless, I felt like a hypocrite. I felt as if I was trying to hide my Christian faith and also missing out on an opportunity to make a difference in someone else's life by testifying and ministering. I could have shared stories of the way God has given me so much love and mercy—starting with my baby, whom I'd been trying to conceive for over a year. God has worked in my life in wonderful ways, and I want to share this with other people.

The biblical writer James stated, 'Anyone who chooses to be a friend of the world becomes an enemy of God' (4:4). What this says to me is not to worry about what people around me think—to serve and please God rather than human beings (see Acts 5:29). And if those around me listen to what I say about the wonders of God, then instead of rejecting him, they'll join in and worship with me.

Prayer: *Dear God, help us to be bold in proclaiming your love and amazing works to those around us. Amen*

Thought for the day: Today I will choose to be a witness to God's presence in my life.

Akua Gite (Texas, US)

Competence from God

Read 2 Corinthians 3:1–5

We are [not] competent in ourselves to claim anything for ourselves, but our competence comes from God.

2 Corinthians 3:5 (NIV)

For most of my life I was full of hubris (excessive pride or self-confidence). My rationale was, 'God has given me abilities and resources, and I honour him by using them to accomplish my tasks.' Never did I ask whether the opportunities and challenges that came my way were in line with God's plan. And even when I failed, I attributed the failure to myself, to my inadequacy. I would eventually ask God for help, but prayer was always my last resort.

Then one day, overwhelmed by the demands on my time and energy, I stopped what I was doing, fell to my knees, and confessed to God that I was helpless. I surrendered my whole being to the Lord, putting everything in his hands. Very quickly, my list of things to do became shorter. From then on, I have tried to listen to and follow God's leading. As a result, I chose to leave corporate work—with its recognition, privileges and pleasures—in favour of working in ministry.

I've learned to attribute the completion of every task, the endurance of every trial, to God. My prayer is that he will give me true humility as exemplified by our Saviour, Jesus Christ (see Philippians 2:1–11).

Prayer: *Loving God, forgive us for our pride. Help us to humble ourselves and to trust fully in you. Amen*

Thought for the day: 'Humble yourselves before the Lord, and he will lift you up' (James 4:10).

Gayla C. Carreon (Quezon City, Philippines)

Getting Rid of Worry

Read Luke 8:4–15

Blessed is the one… whose delight is in the law of the Lord, and who meditates on his law day and night. That person is like a tree planted by streams of water, which yields its fruit in season and whose leaf does not wither—whatever they do prospers.
Psalm 1:1–3 (NIV)

The pink flowers in my garden brought joy to my heart. On the day I planted them, the petals and leaves consumed all the available space. But some time later weeds began to appear, and I was too busy to deal with the problem. By the end of summer, the bed that had once overflowed with colourful flowers was filled with weeds. If only I had maintained the garden and pulled out each weed as it appeared, I would still have an abundance of flowers.

I've noticed that this same phenomenon occurs in my spiritual life. When I ignore the worries that invade my mind, they eventually choke my spiritual growth and the beauty and fragrance of Christ disappear from my life. Like the flowers, I do not mature.

As with weeds, the key is to act when each worry arrives on the scene. I can maintain the soil of my heart by meditating on scripture, since its truth is the best tool for weeding out worry. If I look up verses that speak to the issues that worry me and meditate on those passages, I can be prepared when worry invades my mind. The result will be a life that produces a good crop instead of an abundance of weeds.

Prayer: *Dear Father, thank you for providing a way to cope with worry. Help us to apply your word daily so you can produce abundant fruit in our lives. Amen*

Thought for the day: God's word can help us overcome worry.

Lynn Karidis (Michigan, US)

Be Perfect

Read Colossians 1:24–29

Be perfect, therefore, as your heavenly Father is perfect.
Matthew 5:48 (NIV)

I watched the men laying a new path to my house. They levelled the ground and spread a layer of sand before laying each slab. The builder came and carefully tested the level of each slab.

'Take up those two,' he said. 'We want rainwater to run towards the drain. Let's get the level right.' The men struggled to re-lay the slabs.

'Does it matter?' I observed. 'We're only going to walk on them.'

He looked at me, 'If you don't aim for perfection in the work you do, you'll end up with a poor result,' he said. 'We don't want you tripping up or walking through puddles.'

The apostle Paul was a good workman. He aimed to present his fellow believers 'perfect in Christ'. He needed all the strength that God supplies!

What about my own life? We Christians often shy away from the word 'perfect'. Perhaps we aim for something a little less in our walk with God; but Jesus' words from Matthew 5 are a challenge to us all. Let us go all out to be like our heavenly Father; he will provide us with the strength we need.

Prayer: *Father, you have given me a high calling. Help me to be like you, and aim for perfection in all I do.*

Thought for the day: Let us aim for perfection today.

Marion Turnbull (Liverpool, England)

In God's Image

Read Genesis 1:26–31

Elihu the son of Barachel the Buzite said, 'The spirit of God has made me, and the breath of the Almighty gives me life.'
Job 33:4 (NRSV)

Several years ago, while browsing in an antique shop, my husband and I came across a display of pottery created by a local potter who had made them well over 100 years before. The pieces had been discarded by the potter because they had become misshapen in the firing process. He put the rejected pots on the scrapheap behind his business. Then, over the years, the potter's work became well known, his pottery highly collectable. When the damaged pieces were excavated from the scrapheap, they were considered valuable—not because they were beautiful or even functional but because of who made them.

The story of these pots reminds me of the nature of God's children. We are all misshapen in some way. But each of us is made in the image of God, our creator. As with the pots, our worth does not come from how we look or how functional we are. We are valuable because of who made us.

After viewing the results of creating the world and everything in it, God said that it was very good (see Genesis 1:31). We may sometimes view our fellow humans as less than good. But we are each made in God's image. Our worth, our value comes from him.

Prayer: *Dear Lord, help us to see others through your eyes, remembering that each of us is made in your image. Amen*

Thought for the day: Every single person on earth was created in the image of God.

Mary Jane Hoffmaster (Pennsylvania, US)

How God Heals Us

Read Psalm 6:1–5
I am the Lord, who heals you.
Exodus 15:26 (NIV)

Soon I will be retiring from my job of 43 years. About two months ago I began experiencing health problems that I never had before. I frantically began going from doctor to doctor, taking handfuls of vitamins and other supplements, in the hope that my health would be restored. However, none of my efforts resulted in any improvement.

During the time I was looking for answers for my health problems, I also began searching the scriptures, meditating and praying fervently for God to heal me. But I've come to understand that God does not always answer prayers according to our schedule. In my case, he has shown me that I need to resolve some issues in my life before healing can come.

Now I am diligently working on resolving issues from my past. I have forgiven those who have hurt me and have asked for forgiveness from those whom I have hurt. I am working to clear out all the 'debris' that has been clogging my spiritual life for many years. Whether or not my physical health is restored, I will continue to praise God. Even if I am not healed physically, my spiritual health has been made new.

Prayer: *Dear God of compassion, instil in our minds and hearts that even in the presence of pain, you are beside us holding us in your hands. Amen*

Thought for the day: Even if we are not pain-free, we can be Spirit-filled.

Keith Williams (Alabama, US)

God's Calm Presence

Read 2 Chronicles 15:1–7

Do not be anxious about anything, but in every situation, by prayer and petition, with thanksgiving, present your requests to God.
Philippians 4:6 (NIV)

A problem at work plagued me for two weeks. I looked at every detail, checked every figure, and double-checked all my work. I still had no solution. I walked away from the problem and asked others for help, but I was still stuck. Why was my job so hard?

My title was Budget Analyst, and I analysed every figure as if my life depended on it. I had done everything within my power and knowledge to make the numbers match. Fear of being fired and frustration with my lack of skills weighed heavily on me. I did the only thing left: I got down on my knees.

I thought of Philippians 4:6 and 1 Thessalonians 5:17, which instructed me to pray. Right there in my office, I cried out to God. I put my problem in his hands. I begged for peace, clarity, a solution. I hesitated to go to God with what I considered a trivial problem; but my heart and various Bible verses told me differently. When I got back on my feet, I felt God's calm presence. I knew that whatever happened, I would be OK. Although the solution wasn't immediate (coming a few days later), my heart was immediately filled with peace.

Prayer: *Dear God, teach us in every situation to put our faith and trust in you. Amen*

Thought for the day: Today I will seek God's guidance even for the small things.

Sue Fairchild (Pennsylvania, US)

PRAYER FOCUS: THOSE WHO STRUGGLE IN THEIR JOBS

Embrace the Pain

Read Romans 8:35–39

Consider it pure joy… whenever you face trials of many kinds, because you know that the testing of your faith produces perseverance. Let perseverance finish its work so that you may be mature and complete, not lacking anything.
James 1:2–4 (NIV)

When I was a teenager, my father died suddenly. He was the first person I really and truly loved whom death had taken from me. It was devastating, and I was inconsolable. But as I look back at that event now, I can see the blessings of the Lord on the life of our family in spite of my grief and our loss. While we missed my father terribly, our family grew much closer as a result of his passing. We were able to show our love toward each other in ways we never had while he was alive. The truth was that, in spite of the pain, I became a stronger and better person after my father's death.

Sometimes it seems difficult to have the proper perspective when we are going through a trying time. When we experience a great loss, such as financial ruin or the loss of a significant relationship, we can easily emerge with a broken heart or broken spirit. But to continue to allow our feelings of despair to overwhelm us is neither healthy nor wise. Instead, we can remember the words in today's scripture reading—that God works through distress to bless. Every trial can bring us closer to God—if we let it.

Prayer: *Dear Jesus, help us to embrace the pain of our lives and find you at work even in our grieving. Amen*

Thought for the day: Every test of life can bring us closer to God.

Anthony Collins (Tennessee, US)

Never Alone

Read Isaiah 49:14–15

God said, 'I will never leave you or forsake you.'
Hebrews 13:5 (NRSV)

I have a good friend who offers me comforting advice when I need it. However, since an ocean divides us, I see her only once a year. I often wonder how we remain close despite the time and distance.

The cost of telephoning long distance is expensive, so my friend and I have a one-ring code. When my telephone rings only once, I know my friend is thinking of me. God sends similar signals to me every day. When I hear a kind word from a stranger or I am wrapped in the arms of a loved one, I know that God is with me just as my friend and I remain close in thought.

God's love lives forever in my heart. I have never seen him, yet I know that he is with me always. I know that through my thoughts I can reach him, who hears my prayers and showers me with loving-kindness. I talk to God as I do my friend, and I can sense his presence in the world around me. I am never alone.

Prayer: *Dear God, relieve our worries and cares today. May your love guide us from morning until night, when we lie down in peaceful sleep as we pray, 'Father, hallowed be your name, your kingdom come. Give us each day our daily bread. Forgive us our sins, for we also forgive everyone who sins against us. And lead us not into temptation.' Amen (Luke 11:2–4, NIV)*

Thought for the day: God is with us—always.

Terri Meehan* (Surrey, England)

PRAYER FOCUS: THOSE WHO NEED TO KNOW THAT GOD IS NEAR
* Mrs Meehan died while this issue was in production.

What If?

Read Luke 12:25–30

Jesus said, 'If any want to become my followers, let them deny themselves and take up their cross daily and follow me.'
Luke 9:23 (NRSV)

Many times in life I have tormented myself with 'What if?' questions, asking, 'Where would I be now if only I had made this or that decision?' At other times I worry about the future: 'What if this happens or what if that happens?' This habit often leaves me overwhelmed.

However, I'm coming to see that Jesus does not instruct us to live in the future or the past. We can do very little in this moment about either one. Jesus allows us to live fully in the present, where eternity and our current moment in time meet. I think that when Jesus said, 'take up their cross daily', he meant for us to deal with our present situation, whatever that may be. He tells us to ask for and seek his guidance, 'and follow me'. Jesus Christ is eternal, and from eternity he will shed light on the present situation to show us our way. He may give us only enough clarity and courage to take a single step forward, but it is up to us to 'take up' our present situation and take that step. When we look back, we will see that our whole journey was in Jesus' light.

Prayer: *Dear Lord, please help us to trust in you, that you will guide us through this present time to a glorious eternity. Amen*

Thought for the day: Today, I will follow Jesus—a single step at a time.

Mark Harper Anderson (Pennsylvania, US)

The Transforming Face

Read Matthew 11:28–30

Jesus said, 'Take my yoke upon you and learn from me; for I am gentle and humble in heart, and you will find rest for your souls.'
Matthew 11:29 (NRSV)

'Look into the face of Jesus.' I remember hearing a sermon based on this thought and finding on one occasion it came to my aid in an unexpected way. I was in bed trying to sleep but with no hope of success, as my mind was seething with anger and jealousy, out of control. I tried to look into the face of Jesus, calling up the images of the fair-haired, blue-eyed Jesus of Sunday school books, and the dark-skinned oval face of a Russian icon. It felt like an impossible goal, but it broke the sequence of my whirling thoughts and made the shameful contrast obvious. I fell asleep.

Many years later the same command returned to mind. I wasn't feeling angry, just tired and resentful of the burdens and lack of appreciation arising from my carer's role. But as I tried to look into Jesus' face, I felt a relaxing of my emotional muscles and a wonderful sense of release. Forgiveness was there; both mine for others, and from the source of grace to me. My resentment seemed to dissolve—the yoke became easy, the burden light.

Prayer: *Dear Lord, may the light of your face shine into the dark corners of my soul and make me clean. Amen*

Thought for the day: Turn your face to Jesus and find rest for your soul.

Margaret Gregory (Hertfordshire, England)

A Homesick Scout

Read John 13:34–35

Beloved, since God loved us so much, we also ought to love one another.
1 John 4:11 (NRSV)

I remember one year at Cub Scout summer camp we had a boy who wanted to go home. We were only one day into the week-long camp, but this was his first time away from home. He missed his parents and was always trying to phone them. With the help of camp staff and some older scouts, we managed to convince him to stay at least until Wednesday evening. The older scouts worked really hard to include him in every activity. By Wednesday he had forgotten all about going home.

At first this boy had no desire to be at camp. But the love, care and efforts of the other scouts and adult leaders won him over.

God's love for us is like that boy's experience. God loved us even before we were born. Because of that love we come to know what love is and learn how to share it with all his people. After all, since he loves everyone how can we not try to do the same?

Prayer: *Dear God, we thank you for your love. Help us try to love others as you love them. Amen*

Thought for the day: God's love is abundant—and enough for us all.

Jason Ponzio (Georgia, US)

A Note from God

Read Romans 5:1–5

Be strong, and let your heart take courage, all you who wait for the Lord.
Psalm 31:24 (NRSV)

For many years, I have been battling an eating disorder. Initially, it was a response to teasing in junior school. As I matured and developed a stronger self-image, the disorder faded. After years of feeling I was living a 'healthy' life, my disorder returned—stronger than ever. I was forced to leave my job and go for hospital treatment. After nearly a month and a half in the hospital, then months in intensive outpatient care, I returned home. I still struggle daily to stay on the road to recovery. My days are filled with mental battles, prayers of desperation, attempts to repair injured relationships and, of course, hospital appointments.

I confess I have harboured resentment toward Christians who declare they have heard the voice of God. Then one morning I had my own encounter with him. As I sat in my doctor's waiting room, my eyes were drawn to a scrap of paper lying at my feet. On it were the words: 'Never give up. Never give in.' A message from God? That's what it felt like to me.

I placed this anonymous encouragement where I can see it every day, and I accept with gratitude that God uses many methods to reach us and provide exactly what we need.

Prayer: *O God, thank you for seeking us and showering us with mercy even as we struggle. Strengthen us for our journey. Amen*

Thought for the day: God speaks to us in many, surprising ways.

Amy Grenoble (Pennsylvania, US)

Light for the World

Read Matthew 5:13–16

You are the light of the world. A city on top of a hill can't be hidden.
Matthew 5:14 (CEB)

One morning I sat in my cosy upstairs room overlooking the river—the room where I spend time with God. As I read the scripture verse quoted above, I hoped and prayed that I could be a light to those I would meet and work with that day. Then I looked across the river and noticed a house that stood out from the others. It was bright and shining with a strong light. On looking more closely I could see that it was catching and reflecting the rays of the early-morning sun.

For me, that house was an example of how I could be a light in my world. By being open to the work of the Holy Spirit in me, I can reflect God's light and love in the world. However, I can shine that light into the world only if my relationship with God is a priority. Jesus said, 'I am the light of the world' (John 8:12). When we draw near to Jesus through prayer, Bible study and fellowship with other believers, we can reflect this light to those who do not know him. When we are open and available to the light of Jesus, we—like beacons in a dark world—can shine his love on others.

Prayer: *Heavenly Father, thank you for the light Jesus brings into our lives. May we reflect his light in all we do today. Amen*

Thought for the day: How can I reflect the light of Jesus today?

Ann Stewart (South Australia, Australia)

Doubts

Read Mark 9:14–29

The boy's father exclaimed, 'I do believe; help me overcome my unbelief!'
Mark 9:24 (NIV)

From Moses to Thomas, many people in the Bible experienced moments of doubt. Today's reading tells of a father who brought his son to Jesus to be healed. When Jesus told him, 'Everything is possible for one who believes', the father immediately replied, 'I do believe; help me overcome my unbelief!' I can certainly identify with the inner turmoil that caused the father to confess his doubts and at the same time ask for help with them.

As a young man I went through a period when I struggled in my faith and relationship with God. During this time I also found myself in many difficult, high-stress situations. Because of my doubts, I wondered if God would be willing to help. Nevertheless, I still prayed. I recall once starting a prayer with the words, 'I can't seem to get over these doubts, Lord, but I'm coming to you in spite of them.' Every time I prayed, the strength to endure and carry on seemed to come.

Doubt is not a sin. In fact, honest doubt can be the launching point toward a deep faith. The remedy for doubt is trust and prayer. As I discovered in my doubting time, God is always there. We have only to take that first prayerful step to find rest in his presence.

Prayer: *Dear God, when we are weary with doubts and burdened with unbelief, help us not to give up. Thank you for your constant presence with us. Amen*

Thought for the day: Despite our doubts, God chooses us for service in the world.

Gale A. Richards (Iowa, US)

Outdoor Gifts from God

Read Psalm 19:1–6
The heavens declare the glory of God; the skies proclaim the work of his hands.
Psalm 19:1 (NIV)

My husband and I were towing back to land a small boat containing three stranded fellow fishermen. A short time into the trip, I looked up and was amazed to see overhead a multitude of beautiful orange and black butterflies in migration flight lines that paralleled our route. For over an hour my husband and I marvelled at the delightful creatures gently fluttering toward an unseen winter home.

When we reached land and could talk with the people in the other boat, we exclaimed our joy in being directly under the butterflies the whole trip. The men looked puzzled. They said they had been so focused on their boat that they had never looked up.

That conversation made me wonder if I too am sometimes so consumed by a problem that I don't notice a nearby, lovely blessing from God. As a result, when my soul is troubled, I have learned to pause, to take a wider view and to appreciate the natural beauty God has created for us.

Prayer: *Dear God, when we are distressed, remind us to look beyond ourselves and find comfort in the wonders of your creation. Amen*

Thought for the day: Where do I see God's handiwork today?

Judy Walton (Pennsylvania, US)

Nothing is Impossible!

Read Luke 1:30–37

Jesus… said, 'It's impossible for human beings. But all things are possible for God.'

Matthew 19:26 (CEB)

One of my childhood dreams was to graduate from the University of Nigeria and become a vet. In 2002, I completed high school but couldn't secure an admission into the university. I applied again each of the next three years but to no avail. It seemed as if my dreams were shattered.

As I prepared for the fourth time, something in me remembered prayer, so I decided to cast all my cares on God. As I turned over my problem to him, I had less time to worry about the outcome of my exams. That year, I was admitted, and six years later, I graduated from the University of Nigeria as a veterinary doctor. With God's help, something that had seemed impossible had become a reality.

When the angel told Mary about the birth of the Messiah, Mary asked, 'How will this happen?' The angel told her how, then added, 'Nothing is impossible for God' (Luke 1:34, 37). At times, each of us asks how something will be possible. How can I pay my bills? How can I prevent the foreclosure of my mortgage? How can my son overcome addiction? The angel—and Jesus—reply to us: with God all things are possible, as we cast our cares on him (see 1 Peter 5:7).

Prayer: *Heavenly Father, increase our faith as we learn to trust you more and more with our concerns and our needs. In your Son's name. Amen*

Thought for the day: God can do anything!

Nwakuche Emeka (Imo, Nigeria)

Sirens

Read Psalm 18:1–6

I, the Lord your God, hold your right hand; it is I who say to you, 'Do not fear, I will help you.'
Isaiah 41:13 (NRSV)

As a boy, I was always excited when I heard the sound of a siren. However, later in my life, when I began driving, I often became aggravated with the delay of a few seconds because of an untimely stop or having to wait for an emergency vehicle to pass. Either way, most of the time as soon as the sound was gone, I forgot the incident completely.

Nowadays, I try to think about the way Jesus might view the sound of a siren. Someone is in trouble, possibly in a struggle between life and death. At the very least, someone has been shaken up and is facing expensive car-repair bills. Nearly every time we hear a siren, something bad is happening to someone somewhere.

Today whenever I hear a siren, I pray for those who may be injured. Then I add to my 'siren prayer' a request for the safety of everyone involved, including emergency workers and bystanders. The split-second decisions they make are difficult when the lives or health of others are at stake.

Finally, we can pray for ourselves, that if we encounter an accident or threatening situation before the professionals arrive, we can offer assistance to the victims and pray with them.

Prayer: *Dear Lord, be with those who are in trouble at this moment and need emergency help. Amen*

Thought for the day: Next time I hear a siren, I will pray.

Larry Crockett (Tennessee, US)

Be Quiet!

Read 1 Samuel 3:1–10

Be still, and know that I am God.
Psalm 46:10 (NIV)

My ten-year-old grandson loves to talk, so he often hears this request from his dad: 'Would you please be quiet for just five minutes?' However, he didn't fully understand why his dad needed a break from his constant chatter until he spent an afternoon with his five-year-old cousin, who also loves to talk. My grandson discovered that concentrating on his video game was difficult to do while his little cousin stood beside him, chattering constantly. He finally put down his game, came over to me and said, 'Grandma, now I know why Dad asks me to be quiet for a little while.'

I realised that I too am guilty of being overly talkative when I commune with God. Although I'm generally a quiet person, during my prayers I dominate the conversation, giving God lists of requests and praises. Even while reading my Bible, my thoughts are not always focused on 'listening' to what I'm reading. This makes it difficult for me to comprehend the messages that the Holy Spirit has for me.

God gives us this command in Mark 9:7: 'This is my Son, whom I love. Listen to him!' Therefore, with renewed desire to receive what our Lord has for us to hear, we can say the words of Samuel, 'Speak, for your servant is listening' (1 Samuel 3:10).

Prayer: *Dear Lord, forgive us when we do all of the talking. As we pray, help us to pause and listen to you. Amen*

Thought for the day: Sometimes God's wisdom comes in moments of quiet solitude.

Carol Forehand (Kentucky, US)

Crowding Out Violence

Read 1 John 4:7–12

Love does no wrong to a neighbour.

Romans 13:10 (NRSV)

My wife and I were enjoying a beautiful day at our lakeside home when we received a heartbreaking telephone call from our daughter. The previous evening, she said, our 17-year-old grandson had been the fatal victim of a robbery. We had recently attended his high school graduation, and he had planned to go to college in the autumn. He was a handsome, loving and talented young man. Now, suddenly, he was gone.

In shock, I looked out at the sparkling lake, beautiful trees and green foliage around our home. To me this scene represented the peace that God intends for us. The senseless murder of our grandson was not part of his plan. What, I wondered, led the killers to tear a hole in the glory of God's world? The only answer that came to me was that evil had taken root in their lives because love was not there to crowd it out.

Many people who commit crimes against their neighbours have not experienced God's love through their relationships with others. Much of the violence in life can be prevented if we Christians extend love to all people.

Prayer: *Gracious God, grant us courage to reach out to and love those who do not know you. Amen*

Thought for the day: How can I use my gifts to share God's love with children and young people in need?

Hayes Mizell (South Carolina, US)

From Death to Life

Read 1 Corinthians 15:35–45

Unless a grain of wheat falls into the earth and dies, it remains just a single grain; but if it dies, it bears much fruit.
John 12:24 (NRSV)

Recently, I bought seeds from a garden centre and planted them in pots in my house. While I was doing so, this verse from John 12 came to my mind. I pondered how planting seeds is similar to what Jesus said—that the seed must die, meaning the seed must be buried before it can bear fruit. These words were fulfilled in Jesus' life. He died on the cross and was buried for three days. Through his death, the Word of God was sown in everyone who believed in him, and those people proclaimed it to other people. The death of Jesus produced—and continues to produce—much fruit.

Currently, the number of Christians is over two billion, or one-third of the world's population. All this is the result of Jesus' sacrifice on the cross. Whenever I take Holy Communion, I want to reflect on how Jesus willingly sacrificed and, like a little grain of wheat, was buried so that the fruit of faith, love and hope could be produced in countless lives.

Prayer: *Dear Lord Jesus, thank you for dying and rising from the dead so that we can live for ever with you. Amen*

Thought for the day: Christ died so that we can live.

David Nababan (Jakarta, Indonesia)

One Simple Prayer

Read Romans 8:18–28

We know that all things work together for good for those who love God, who are called according to his purpose.

Romans 8:28 (NRSV)

My husband had returned from visiting his father who was in intensive care at a hospital three hours' drive away. My father-in-law had been ill for 18 years and now seemed finally to be dying. After my family had gone to bed, I sat down to reflect on the stressful events of the day.

I prayed for my husband and for other family members who had stayed behind at the hospital. But when I tried to pray for my father-in-law, I realised that I did not know how to pray for him. I couldn't think of what to say, so I prayed for God's will for him. I thanked God that I could pray that simple prayer in all situations and trusted that God would work all things for good (see Romans 8:28).

I picked up *The Upper Room* and turned to that day's meditation. The first words I read were: Jesus prayed, 'Thy kingdom come. Thy will be done…' (Matthew 6:10, KJV). The verse was exactly what I needed to confirm that God had heard my prayer. I immediately felt peace and a renewed connection with God. I knew that he understood and had received my prayer.

Prayer: *Dear God, thank you for Jesus' example of a perfect prayer. Help us to come before you with our burdens and concerns as we pray, 'Our Father in heaven, hallowed be your name, your kingdom come, your will be done, on earth as it is in heaven. Give us today our daily bread. And forgive us our debts, as we also have forgiven our debtors. And lead us not into temptation, but deliver us from the evil one.'* Amen*

Thought for the day: God hears our prayers, even when we have no words.

Cathy Lee Taylor (Florida, US)

Leaving by Another Door

Read John 8:1–11

Jesus said, 'Let any one of you who is without sin be the first to throw a stone at her.'
John 8:7 (NIV)

The fancy-dress party was enjoyed by all. Everyone, from the tiniest baby to the oldest grandfather, donned a disguise. There were games, food and lots of fun. Toward the end of the evening, the organiser thanked everyone, especially those of us who had helped with the event. We waited to clean up as the boys and girls and their mums filed out in high spirits. The dads left by another door to return to their prison cells.

We volunteers are members of the local community; most of us are members of Christian churches. Sad to say, not all members of our local community approve of what we are doing. In fact, some are quite hostile toward the prisoners because of the wrong they have done. However, as our Bible reminds us, none of us is free from sin. Through Christ, we know that we have been forgiven, and we want to extend that love and acceptance to others. We hope and pray that we can help to convince the prisoners and their families of God's love for them.

Prayer: *Dear Lord, help us to help other people in kind and non-judgemental ways. Amen*

Thought for the day: How can I share God's love with others?

William Findlay (Glasgow, Scotland)

Loving Relationships

Read Matthew 22:34–40

Jesus said to the lawyer, 'You shall love the Lord your God with all your heart, and with all your soul, and with all your mind… You shall love your neighbour as yourself.'

Matthew 22:37–39 (NRSV)

As a retired scientist, I am enjoying taking a course on the history of science. I was intrigued by the instructor's statement that one of the most important scientific ideas to emerge in the 20th century showed that all reality—from the atom to the universe—can be understood in terms of relationships. As a Christian, I was fascinated to learn that a concept that runs throughout the Old and New Testaments has a parallel in the latest scientific thinking.

Humans are spiritual and physical beings. Our relationship with God is our primary concern, and our relationships with other humans second only to that. Cultivating both these kinds of relationships is a lifelong challenge, requiring our constant attention.

How thankful we can be that God through Christ graciously offers us forgiveness when we fail to maintain our relationships with God and others! Only in his commandments do we find our ultimate reality in this life and in the life to come.

Prayer: *Lord Jesus Christ, help us to obey your commandments of love and remain in right relationship with you and others. Amen*

Thought for the day: How will I make time for my relationship with God and with others today?

Richard Gillum (Maryland, US)

God Sees, Hears, Loves

Read James 5:13–18

Are any among you suffering? They should pray. Are any cheerful? They should sing songs of praise.
James 5:13 (NRSV)

I confess that prayer is not the strongest of my spiritual disciplines. I am comfortable leading prayers in worship or praying for someone who is ill. But making a disciplined effort to spend a good amount of time in prayer is very difficult for me. I get anxious when I sit still; my mind is not one that easily goes quiet.

But that day was important. My husband had a big job interview, and we were both anxious. From the time he left the house until the time he returned, I prayed for him. I prayed through my morning routine of showering and dressing. I prayed while I brewed my coffee, and then I sat on the sofa for an hour and poured my heart out to the Lord in intercession for my husband. It was an emotionally draining experience, but I believe it was the very best way I could have cared for my spouse.

It isn't necessarily the way we pray that matters or whether we sit, kneel or stand. It isn't about whether we speak out loud in narrative or make lists, or say one-word prayers throughout the day. What matters most is that we do pray, intentionally and faithfully, pouring out all our joys and fears to God, who sees all, hears all, loves all.

Prayer: *Friend and Redeemer, thank you for the opportunity to communicate with you through prayer. Help us to find ways throughout the day to communicate with you. Amen*

Thought for the day: What matters most is not how, when or where we pray but that we pray.

Loren Tate Mitchell (Virginia, US)

Hand-Me-Downs

Read Colossians 3:12–17

Renew the thinking in your mind by the Spirit and clothe yourself with the new person created according to God's image in justice and true holiness.

Ephesians 4:23–24 (CEB)

When I was growing up, children wore hand-me-downs: clothes, often darned or patched, passed down from older brothers and sisters. Except at school, at church and for special occasions, I often wore clothing that no longer fitted my brother. I wore what my parents provided. Some hand-me-downs were better than others.

I also wore attitudes, behaviour, beliefs and responses that were handed down—received from my parents and other role models. Some were good and acceptable; others were not.

When I grew up and started to earn a living, I cast off my drab hand-me-downs, bought new clothes, and took responsibility for what I wore.

On the glorious day when I asked Jesus into my life, I prayerfully sorted through my spiritual and behavioural hand-me-downs and asked God to take away my soiled, broken and destructive behaviour, beliefs and attitudes and to clothe me anew in the Spirit.

Prayer: *Dear Lord, please grant us forgiveness, strength and grace to put aside hurtful attitudes, speech and actions. Adorn us with the bright clothing of faith and love. Amen*

Thought for the day: Today I will take time to think before I speak or act.

Keith Honeyman (Western Cape, South Africa)

No Source Signal

Read Isaiah 9:1–7

Surely God is my salvation; I will trust and not be afraid. The Lord, the Lord himself, is my strength and my defence; he has become my salvation.
Isaiah 12:2 (NIV)

I was going through a difficult time. My husband and I had divorced after 15 years of marriage. Then a year later he was killed in a motorcycle accident. I was struggling to keep myself and our teenage son going. My faith in God was strong; but the day-to-day challenges of single parenthood, financial insecurity and grief were taking their toll. Spending time with God had moved further down my to-do list.

A friend asked me to join her women's Bible study group. Studying Isaiah 30:15 taught me the importance of listening for God's direction: 'In repentance and rest is your salvation, in quietness and trust is your strength.' I found comfort and strength as I renewed my relationship with God. How immediate and accessible is our God! Joining a Bible study helped to correct my priorities and to connect me with our all-powerful, all-knowing and ever-present Lord.

Prayer: *Dear God, forgive us when the demands of daily life become our idols. Help us always to put you first and to listen closely and quietly for your guidance. Amen*

Thought for the day: How am I connecting to God, my source of strength, today?

Sara S. Orellana (Florida, US)

Christ's Love for Us

Read Ephesians 3:13–21

My lips praise you because your faithful love is better than life itself!
Psalm 63:3 (CEB)

Yesterday in church I observed the family sitting in front of me. The son sat in a wheelchair beside the parents. He was throwing his head back and forth intensely, incessantly. As soon as they sat down, the father stretched out his arm, leaned his elbow against the wheelchair handle, and held the back of the boy's head to calm the spasms. Throughout the sermon, I saw how the father's hand held and caressed the boy's head. Finally, the boy was pacified by his father's touch; his head became still.

For me, the image of this father and son was a sermon in itself. The love that the father expressed was so patient, so enduring and so great that I'm sure it came from God, transported through the father to his son. It seemed to me that the father realised that God had given him so much love for his son that it overcame the hardships of having a child with special needs. In that moment, the father opened up his heart for Christ's love to flow through him.

Prayer: *God of all comfort, help us to be a conduit for your love. Amen*

Thought for the day: Today I will clear my heart of anything that stands in the way of Christ's love.

Agneta Johansson (Jönköping, Sweden)

Ash Wednesday

Read Isaiah 58:1–12

God said, 'Is not this the fast that I choose: to loose the bonds of injustice…? Is it not to share your bread with the hungry, and bring the homeless poor into your house?'
Isaiah 58:6–7 (NRSV)

I have always thought of Lent as a time of fasting in the sense of 'giving up' something, either a lunch or some daily treat such as chocolate or coffee. The customary question in my church community is, 'What are you giving up for Lent?' I had never thought about doing anything else as a Lenten practice until one morning when I read the passage above from Isaiah, and later that same morning I encountered a divine example of that passage.

While I was driving to work I noticed a drably-dressed, bearded man standing on the pavement. He held a sign that read: 'Homeless—need help'. Instantly, I recalled the words of Isaiah about what kind of fast God desires: 'to share your bread with the hungry, and bring the homeless poor into your house'. I gave what help I could to that man.

My Lenten practice changed that very day. Now during Lent, my practice is not to give up something but to give something to someone in need.

Prayer: *Dear Lord, help us during this Lenten season to look beyond ourselves and give to those in need. In Jesus' name we pray. Amen*

Thought for the day: When we fast, God helps us to identify with—and reach out to—those in need.

Edward L. Kelly, Jr (Iowa, US)

Jesus Loves Me

Read 2 Corinthians 4:15–18
We do not lose heart. Though outwardly we are wasting away, yet inwardly we are being renewed day by day.
2 Corinthians 4:16 (NIV)

My mother-in-law hadn't spoken in several months; at least, she hadn't spoken words we could decipher. The ravages of Alzheimer's disease had taken over her mind and body. We often wondered what she was thinking, what she felt deep inside.

One evening, my husband and I were taking turns to feed his mother her dinner. As we sat with her, I began to sing softly, 'Jesus loves me! This I know.' For an instant, her face brightened and she nodded her head. 'Yes, that's right,' she said clearly, the way she had spoken years before.

It lasted for only a moment, but that was enough. My mother-in-law couldn't feed herself. She couldn't speak. She didn't even know who we were. But deep in her soul, Jesus' love continued to sustain her. Nothing—not even Alzheimer's disease—'will be able to separate us from the love of God that is in Christ Jesus our Lord' (Romans 8:39).

Prayer: *Dear God, help us to see your love even in the most difficult situations. In Christ's name, we pray. Amen*

Thought for the day: Nothing can separate us from the love of God.

Nancy C. Todd (Kentucky, US)

Learning Through a Child

Read Luke 18:15–17

Jesus called them and said, 'Let the little children come to me, and do not stop them; for it is to such as these that the kingdom of God belongs.'
Luke 18:16 (NRSV)

Crash! Our six-year-old grandson has 'fallen' off his chair in the middle of prayer time. 'Not again,' I groan inwardly. Knowing only too well this is no accident, my husband and I frown at him with disapproval, unlike the people on the back row who turn anxiously to ask if he's hurt and give him a reassuring smile.

He enjoys coming to church with us and usually sits at a little table at the back to draw and write. We sit near enough for him to come to us if he needs to. Most of the time he pretends not to be listening, but we are not fooled—we know he soaks up everything like a sponge! We love our grandson dearly; we give him comfort and encouragement, answer his questions and are always ready to forgive him—but we also have to discipline him when necessary.

In this I see a picture of God's constant love for me, his precious child. Many times he needs to discipline me when I am wayward, but he is always ready to forgive me when I repent, and to comfort and reassure me when I need it. He encourages me to turn to Jesus, my Saviour and Lord, with childlike trust, and to grow step by step as I learn from him. I know I can take my questions to him and speak to him in my prayers. I can put my hand in his and be sure I am accepted and safe—because I am his dearly loved child.

Prayer: *Dear Lord Jesus, thank you for your complete understanding of us, and for accepting, forgiving, loving, teaching and encouraging us. Help us to allow you to change us and make us more like you. Amen*

Thought for the day: We can learn lessons from our children and grandchildren.

Julie Rawles (Somerset, England)

Excess Baggage

Read Isaiah 43:18–19
Cast all your anxiety on [God] because he cares for you.
1 Peter 5:7 (NIV)

Last year we experienced two quite different holidays, one by car and one by plane. As we packed for our plane journey, weight restrictions and bag sizes challenged us. We were used to travelling in our old car with plenty of room, so we could take much paraphernalia. But for the plane travel, we had to be very particular—weighing each article and packing and repacking our suitcases until they were under the required weight. This made us much more aware of which items were really necessary to take with us.

God is showing me that just as on our car holidays, I drag along unnecessary things on my life's journey. I think I'll need them; but in reality they are baggage from the past, habits that I don't need, thoughts that flood my mind and weigh down my spirit.

Becoming Christians means we are to start a new life—parting with our old life and our old ways. Gradually, as we pay attention, we can see God's Holy Spirit revealing our destructive attitudes and habits. This process frees up space in our minds and hearts to fill with the freedom that Christ—through his suffering—has won for us.

Prayer: *Dear heavenly Father, help us listen to your Holy Spirit to discern the old ways we need to get rid of and give us strength to let go of them. In Jesus' name. Amen*

Thought for the day: Instead of being weighed down by old baggage, I can be free in Christ.

Lenore Warton (New South Wales, Australia)

What's In a Name?

Read Exodus 3:1–14

God said to Moses, 'I am who I am. This is what you are to say to the Israelites: "I am has sent me to you."'

Exodus 3:14 (NIV)

In the Hebrew Bible, names represent hopes, dreams and the characteristics of people. For example, Jacob, after wrestling with an angel, was given a new name, Israel, which means 'the one who struggled with God'. Knowing the name of a person can give insight into the origin, nature and the dreams of the person and his or her family.

That's why Moses asked God this question: What is your name? Knowing God's name could tell us many things about him!

God said, 'I am who I am!' In some translations, God said, 'I shall be who I shall be.' Both translations are possible because the Hebrew grammar allows for both translations ('to be' or 'to become'). When God says 'I am who I am' he is actually refusing to be defined by one word. He is saying, 'I am free. I am not defined. I am the Creator, not the created.' When God said, 'I shall be who I shall be,' he was saying, 'I am the one who causes things to be. I am the Creator of history.'

Though we may want to define God more narrowly, knowing that he is 'I am who I am' can give us more confidence in him. God is free, undefined and is present in all aspects of our lives.

Prayer: *Dear God, thank you for the gift of creation and the limitless gift of your presence with us. Amen*

Thought for the day: How do my names for God limit my faith?

Sungho Lee (California, US)

Choosing Forgiveness

Read Genesis 33:1–4

Brothers and sisters, if a person is caught doing something wrong, you who are spiritual should restore someone like this with a spirit of gentleness.

Galatians 6:1 (CEB)

As I listened to our pastor confess his greatest sin and failure, I felt shock, disbelief and disappointment. Then, suddenly, I was overwhelmed by a more powerful feeling. My heart burned with compassion and mercy. I had been given a glimpse of God's heart. As the pastor stood before us, pleading for forgiveness, the words were whispered in my spirit: 'You are forgiven.'

We are children living in a fallen world; we all fall short. How do we respond when our brothers and sisters sin?

Genesis provides a beautiful illustration of a brother's love and forgiveness. Jacob had stolen Esau's inheritance and blessing. Many years later, when the brothers were reunited, Esau made a choice. He could have held on to resentment, but he chose to receive his brother with grace and mercy.

Faced with the transgressions of our fellow believers, we can choose to be bitter and to blame them. Or we can choose to reach out with loving arms to lift up our brothers and sisters when they stumble.

Prayer: *Merciful God, thank you for your unending grace. Thank you for loving us no matter how many times we fail. Help us to extend your love to our brothers and sisters. Amen*

Thought for the day: How can I offer the grace of Christ to fellow believers?

Mari Leigh Fanning (Alabama, US)

Where We Don't Want to Go

Read Matthew 26:36–46

When you are old you will stretch out your hands, and someone else will dress you and lead you where you do not want to go.
John 21:18 (NIV)

Recently my mum endured several hospital stays and a period in a nursing home for recuperation. Though weak, she still managed sparks of wry humour. One afternoon as I fastened her hospital gown, she smiled and said, 'I really can relate to that verse about someone else dressing you and taking you where you don't want to go.'

Later, I pondered Jesus' words to Peter in John 21:18. Like Mum, we all occasionally face circumstances over which we have no control. What do we do? Jesus' next words offer the solution: 'Follow me' (John 21:19). Jesus left an example for us to follow (see 1 Peter 2:21). How did he handle the prospect of unavoidable pain and suffering? What did he do when he knew what was necessary but still hoped for a way out?

To answer these questions God led me to Matthew 26:36–46. Jesus' time in the Garden of Gethsemane reveals four steps he took that we can follow. First, we can pray, and then pray again. Then, we can accept what cannot be changed. Next we can submit control to God. Finally, we can step out in faith, assured that God will go with us.

Prayer: *Dear Lord, in the circumstances we are powerless to change, help us to relinquish control to you. Amen*

Thought for the day: In tough times, I will remember to pray and step out in faith.

Pamela Williams (Pennsylvania, US)

Keeping the Sabbath

Read Mark 2:23—3:6

[Jesus] said to [the Pharisees], 'The sabbath was made for humankind, and not humankind for the sabbath.'
Mark 2:27 (NRSV)

We were driving to church one Sunday morning when my dad made a turn in the opposite direction. I asked where we were going, and he told me we were going to worship God in a different way that day. Always up for something new, I was excited about this adventure. He explained that we were on our way to visit his friend's grandmother. Since his friend had moved away there was really no family to visit her. For the next hour we sat in a small flat that had a distinct musty odour, spending time with a deeply appreciative and lonely woman. When we left my dad promised to return.

That happened over 30 years ago. After that initial visit, my dad continued to visit her regularly. He would talk to her, do odd jobs and sometimes do some shopping if she needed it.

My dad showed me another way among many to worship God and taught me that worship does not have to be limited to a church service. Worship in church is important because it is done in a community that loves God and wants to express that love. That is exactly what my father and I did when we visited this woman. We shared God's love with her. It is the same lesson that Christ demonstrated; helping those in need is always a good option.

Prayer: *Dear God, help us to keep the sabbath in our deeds by remembering that we are to love others because you first loved us. Amen*

Thought for the day: What is a new way I can worship God today?

Matthew L. Reger (Ohio, US)

God Empowers

Read Jeremiah 1:4–10

Surely I know the plans I have for you, says the Lord, plans for your welfare and not for harm, to give you a future with hope.
Jeremiah 29:11 (NRSV)

After ten years out of the job market, I was invited to get involved with a group of people to develop fundraising projects to benefit the community. The group was composed of a social worker, a psychologist, an educational psychologist and me, a psychology student. Among these colleagues I often felt small and unprepared for the challenges.

In moments of weakness, we are tempted to let our insecurities and limitations grow. Suffering generates anxiety, and we end up hiding our potential and withdrawing from the opportunities God has in store for us.

What a relief to know that God has plans for us, plans for our welfare and not for evil and distress! Knowing that God trusts us gives us the strength and courage to face our challenges and to realise our potential and our gifts. 'In all these things we are more than conquerors through him who loved us' (Romans 8:37).

Prayer: *Thank you, God. Even when we doubt our abilities, you hold us in your loving arms and show us how capable we are. Amen*

Thought for the day: We are all capable because God empowers us.

Esmar Ferreira (Fortaleza, Brazil)

PRAYER FOCUS: SOMEONE WITH A NEW JOB

Behind Prison Walls

Read Philippians 2:12–18

Do everything without grumbling or arguing, so that you may become blameless and pure, 'children of God without fault in a warped and crooked generation'. Then you will shine among them like stars in the sky as you hold firmly to the word of life.

Philippians 2:14–16 (NIV)

Nearly four years ago I began counselling prisoners in alcohol rehabilitation. I tell these men about what Jesus has done for me; I am a recovering alcoholic with over 20 years of sobriety.

Most of the inmates are serving long sentences for murder or armed robbery. However, my colleagues and I seldom hear foul language, and the men are genuinely happy to be with us. They never complain about having to spend 23 hours each day locked up in a small cell. We don't hear complaints about the food or about the lack of air conditioning in summer. They never speak about the harshness of prison warders or stringent prison rules.

What we do hear over and over again is this question: 'Why do you drive 40 miles to spend your evening with us, of all people?' We explain to them that we can't keep what God has given us—sobriety and a future—unless we in turn give it away. We want to share the good news of God's love with them as well. We tell the prisoners we also come to learn the lessons they can teach us. Already we have learned not to complain and to be grateful for all that we have.

Prayer: *O God, teach us to be grateful for the ways you care for your people, whether we are inside or outside prison walls. Amen*

Thought for the day: What have I thanked God for today?

Scott Wierenga (Michigan, US)

Accepting Change

Read Isaiah 43:1–7

I am convinced that neither death nor life, neither angels nor demons, neither the present nor the future, nor any powers, neither height nor depth, nor anything else in all creation, will be able to separate us from the love of God that is in Christ Jesus our Lord.
Romans 8:38–39 (NIV)

When I was younger, I welcomed change. That was probably because I either instigated the changes in my life or at least seemed to have control over them. Life was full of new possibilities as I went off to college, learned new things and made new friends. Change was everywhere, encouraged and embraced.

Now that I am older, I realise that life sometimes leads me to places I don't want to go. I have become resistant to change and often try to cling to the status quo. My head knows that this is impossible but my heart remains stubborn.

We often don't see 'the big picture' in life; only God does. Change can bring about anxiety and fear, until we recognise that God is with us in the midst of all change.

Letting go of fear begins when we trust in God. When change comes, we can ask what we can learn from the situation. We can look for what God might be trying to teach us, which can lessen our resistance to change. And we can pray that we will be able to cope with change and allow God to guide us through it.

Prayer: *O God, walk with us today and be our guide through whatever changes may come. Amen*

Thought for the day: Fear decreases as faith increases.

Michael Arnum (Massachusetts, US)

Epiphany

In recent years, I have noticed that instead of making new year's resolutions many people are choosing a word for the year—a word to help them focus, to motivate them, to shape their thinking through the year. I know people who have chosen words like love, peace, slow and fun.

I first experienced this practice during a celebration of Epiphany when my college chaplain passed around a basket of gold paper stars, each with a word written on one side. As the basket was passed, each person took out a star. 'This is your Epiphany star,' the chaplain said. 'Let this word guide and shape your day, your week, or even your year. What might God teach you through this word?' When my turn came, I pulled out a star that read 'contentment'. At the time I had just begun attending college and was homesick, missing my family and friends. 'Contentment?' I thought. 'Am I supposed to be content with this loneliness?'

As I pondered my Epiphany word and lived with its challenge, I began to see several meanings to contentment. Contentment was a challenge: how could I work to find a place of contentment with my situation? Contentment was a prayer—that I would find the friendships and community to support me and help me be at peace with my life. It was also a call to action: what should I not be content to accept as it was? What changes did I need to make in my life, my attitude, my world? Living with that Epiphany star of contentment for a year taught me much about myself and brought me closer to God through prayer and discernment.

Our chaplain's decision to give us these stars at Epiphany was no accident. The word epiphany is from the Greek word 'epiphaneia', meaning 'manifestation' or 'striking appearance'. An epiphany is a moment when a person suddenly sees or understands something in a new or very clear way. Those Epiphany stars invited us to look for new understanding in our lives.

The Christian celebration of Epiphany is another such invitation. At Epiphany we celebrate the visit of the magi to the Christ child, the promised Messiah. Christ's holy nature was revealed to them as they knelt before him. This story invites us to understand our world in a new way. God has entered into human life, and everything has changed. We, like the wise men, can see and experience the Holy One—if we are paying attention.

At this time of year we remember another epiphany story—the presentation of Jesus in the temple (see Luke 2:22–38). Following Jewish practice, Joseph and Mary presented baby Jesus in the temple. He was received by Simeon and Anna, two faithful people who had devoted their lives to prayer and were open to the workings of the Holy Spirit. They recognised Jesus as '[God's] salvation' and 'a light for revelation to the Gentiles and for glory to [the] people [of] Israel' (Luke 2:30, 32, NRSV). Even without the trappings of the manger, the heavenly host of angels, and wise men bearing precious gifts, they recognised the divine when they encountered it.

Throughout the Church year, Christ appears to us again and again. Jesus' baptism, the wedding in Cana, each story of healing, each act of love, each parable Jesus teaches reveal God's divine presence on earth. God appears again and again, and it is up to us to pay attention, to remain ready to encounter him all around us.

So this year, my word is epiphany. Through prayerful and intentional focus on epiphany, I will watch for the ways God is working in my life and in the world. I will be motivated to acts of love, compassion, peace and justice as God appears in striking ways. I will shape my thinking to expect epiphany—the appearance of the divine in daily life that suddenly gives me a new vision and understanding of who God is calling me to be.

As you consider Epiphany and what word you might choose to shape your thinking this year, you may wish to read again the meditations for January 4, 8, 12, 24, 26 and 31; February 15, 18, 19 and 28; March 8, 20 and 31; and April 2, 14 and 23.

Questions for Reflection

1. What word will focus, motivate or inspire you in 2015? Why did you choose this word?

2. Where have you encountered God recently? Describe the experience. How did that experience change your understanding of yourself, of the world or of God?

Lindsay Gray is a graduate of Hollins University where she received a bachelor's degree in religious studies and developed a passion for writing and editing. In 2012, after receiving her Master of Divinity degree, she joined the staff of The Upper Room. In her work as managing editor, she particularly enjoys collaborating with writers, helping them share their experiences of God in clear and relatable ways. Lindsay lives in Nashville, Tennessee with her husband, Dawson. Her hobbies include horseback riding, knitting and playing board games.

Living Bread and Water

Read John 6:25–35

Jesus said to them, 'I am the bread of life. Whoever comes to me will never be hungry, and whoever believes in me will never be thirsty.'
John 6:35 (NRSV)

'Are you hungry? Are you thirsty?' Our mother always asked us these questions the moment we came in the back door after playing in the hot summer sun. If we said 'no', the next response was 'Are you sure?'

Regardless of our situation or circumstances in the world, these questions face us all. For all humans and creatures, paying attention to physical hunger and thirst is essential. But hunger and thirst can also apply to spiritual realities. There are deserts where people find themselves emotionally, intellectually and spiritually bankrupt. In those places, pain, longing and danger lurk. Temptations abound which offer temporary relief from hunger and thirst. There are many 'things' that could feed us or quench our thirst.

Yet in the midst of these places of temptation, Jesus' words resound, 'I am the bread of life. Whoever comes to me will never be hungry, and whoever believes in me will never be thirsty.'

We are assured throughout scripture that there are no places where we find ourselves where Jesus is not present. In the midst of the worst hungers of our lives, we are not alone. God is there saying 'I am with you.' We are assured that no matter where we find ourselves God is there—offering water to our thirsty spirits and food for our desperately hungry hearts.

Prayer: *Gracious God, thank you for offering bread and water to our hungry and thirsting bodies. Amen*

Thought for the day: God meets us in every situation of our lives and offers living bread and water.

Karen Greenwaldt (North Carolina, US)

Joy in Preaching Christ

Read Philippians 1:12–30

I eagerly expect and hope that I will in no way be ashamed, but will have sufficient courage so that now as always Christ will be exalted in my body, whether by life or by death. For to me, to live is Christ and to die is gain.

Philippians 1:20–21 (NIV)

Recently, I've been thinking about Paul's letter to the church in Philippi. While imprisoned for preaching Christ, Paul expressed joy in the knowledge that the gospel of the love and saving grace of Jesus Christ was being preached, regardless of the manner in which the message was relayed. Rather than seek sympathy for his unjust imprisonment or vengeance against those stirring up trouble for him, Paul declares that no matter what happens he will continue to rejoice.

Paul's experience and testimony have made me look back at my own life as a Christian believer and ask myself if I glorify Christ in life as Paul did. Unlike the apostle Paul, when trouble comes along I am more likely to shy away and seek sympathy from others. Likewise, I am more inclined to seek revenge against those from whom the trouble comes.

How I wish and pray for courage to emulate Paul! I want to find joy in every circumstance, knowing that Christ is being preached through my life, both in happy moments and during the times of my sufferings.

Prayer: *Thank you, Lord, for Paul's example of what it means to serve you in all circumstances. Give us the strength to rejoice and preach the gospel through our happy moments and in sad ones too. Amen*

Thought for the day: How am I reflecting Christ through my life?

Philip Polo (Nairobi, Kenya)

Working for Good

Read Romans 8:26–32

Praise be to… the God of all comfort, who comforts us in all our troubles, so that we can comfort those in any trouble with the comfort we ourselves receive from God.
2 Corinthians 1:3–4 (NIV)

When I was diagnosed with cancer, people started to pray for me—missionaries, church friends and relatives. That was two years ago last month. As time went by, I wondered why God had sustained my life. Surely God must have a job that I should be doing! My previous service was in places like Kenya, Uganda, Ecuador and Poland but, I reasoned, I couldn't do anything like that now that I had cancer.

Last month I had the privilege to go back to my home town, and I think I have discovered my job. I found so many of my friends to be disabled, in pain, in hospital or nursing homes, or suffering from just growing old. I stayed four weeks and was blessed to be able to visit these friends, help them in and out of cars, go to lunch or just enjoy a telephone call. I may have cancer, but I do not have any pain or disability—either physical or mental. What a blessing I received from my friends! Now that I am back at home, I will continue my volunteer job of driving cancer patients to their appointments. I feel truly blessed that God has directed me to this new area of service.

Prayer: *Dear God, help us to remember that all things work together for good to those who love you and who are called for your purpose. Amen*

Thought for the day: On any day, if I look around, I will find someone to help.

Jean Glick (Florida, US)

Reconnecting with Christ

Read Matthew 6:1–6

When you fast, put oil on your head and wash your face, so that your fasting may be seen not by others but by your Father who is in secret.
Matthew 6:17–18 (NRSV)

I am thankful for the season of Lent. Why? A few years ago, I found something that, over time, I had lost. I found Jesus Christ.

One Sunday before Ash Wednesday, our minister challenged us to search prayerfully from within about how to observe Lent. He wanted us to understand this time of reflection, penitence and fasting on a personal level. He explained that penitence is often practised through fasting or self-denial. I decided to deny myself 'my time'—time after breakfast that usually consisted of playing computer games or reading a newspaper. I replaced that time with devotions: reading, studying, praying and meditating. I began to relearn the books of the Bible. I found scripture passages and lessons I had once known but had forgotten over time.

In the beginning when I gave up 'my time', I thought I was really sacrificing. But instead I realised that previously I had been sacrificing the knowledge of eternal life. Lent is a time for reflection on Jesus—his life, sacrificial death and resurrection. That first year, my sacrifice allowed me to reconnect with Christ. Since then, it has allowed me to grow closer to him each day.

Prayer: *God of life, we praise you for the gift of your Son. Help us to find ways to grow closer to him every day. Amen*

Thought for the day: What am I doing to grow closer to Christ?

Janet Pierce (Tennessee, US)

Learning to Receive

Read John 13:1–8
'God opposes the proud, but gives grace to the humble.'
1 Peter 5:5 (NRSV)

At the time, I was convinced I was doing the honourable Christian thing. After all, the Bible says that it's better to give than to receive (Acts 20:35). I thought turning down my friend's offer of food was part of learning 'in whatsoever state I am, therewith to be content' (Philippians 4:11, KJV).

Kind-hearted enough not to take 'no' for an answer, that same friend blessed me the very next day with a bag of groceries. Included were foods that I had been wanting to taste but could never afford.

Still accustomed to being the 'giver', I insisted that he give the groceries to someone who 'really' needed them. But when he left the gift on my table, it was clear that God had told him that I was the one who needed them.

While enjoying the food, I remembered Peter's rejection of Jesus' desire to serve him by washing his tired feet. Suddenly it sank in; I was a mirror image of the prideful apostle. Brought up to be self-sufficient, I viewed letting others do something for me as a sign of weakness. As I meditated further on the scriptures, the Holy Spirit blessed me with wonderful enlightenment: part of serving others is letting them serve me.

Prayer: *Dear heavenly Father, help us to understand that being willing to receive is itself an act of love for another. In Jesus' name. Amen*

Thought for the day: The Lord of lords wants to serve me; will I let him?

Antoine J. Murphy (Wisconsin, US)

One Big Family

Read Ephesians 2:11–22
Through [Christ] we… have access to the Father by one Spirit.
Ephesians 2:18 (NIV)

Perhaps the greatest blessing I receive from reading *The Upper Room* is my awareness of how vast the Christian community is around the world. Often after reading a meditation written by a fellow Christian on the other side of the globe from me, I sit silently in awe that I have a sister or brother in Christ in that location. I am overwhelmed by the knowledge that we are united by the same heavenly Father, even though great distances separate us. I am humbled by the privilege of joining with millions of Christians around the world in the prayer focus for the day.

Too often we think of the church as only the Christians in our local congregation, our town or our denomination, when it is so much more. Jesus knew the need of people everywhere to hear the good news when he sent out his disciples to teach (see Matthew 28:19). While clearly much work remains to be done, it is also clear that the good news has been shared far and wide.

Every day I join in the prayer at the close of the meditation. And I pray for the writer who is my sister or brother in Christ, wherever he or she lives.

Prayer: *God of all the world, pour out your blessing, pressed down and overflowing, upon your children everywhere (see Luke 6:38). Amen*

Thought for the day: Prayer connects us to the worldwide family of God.

Madeline Peterson (Nebraska, US)

Trusting God Always

Read Isaiah 55:6–9

Jesus looked at them carefully and said, 'It's impossible for human beings. But all things are possible for God.'
Matthew 19:26 (CEB)

Recently, my daughter and I were both ill while my husband was in another town for his work. So, when we needed some medicine we had no one to go to the pharmacy in the village to buy it for us. I prayed, 'Lord, please send someone to help us.' Soon after my prayer, I heard footsteps coming toward our house. When she entered the house, I recognised a girl who lives nearby. This girl can hardly speak, and she doesn't know how to read or write. However, I smiled at her as she came to me, realising that she was being sent by God to tend to our needs that day. I took a piece of paper, wrote down the name of the medicine that we needed, and gave her some money. I asked her to go to the pharmacy and then bring the medicine back to the house. To my relief, she returned to the house only 20 minutes later with the medicine in her hand.

I realised that even though I thought it was impossible to ask that girl for help at that time, God made it possible for her to understand and for me to trust. God's ways are truly far greater than our ways. He is faithful and will never abandon us.

Prayer: *Dear Lord, help us to realise that your love and ways are greater than our ways and expectations. Amen*

Thought for the day: Everything is possible with God.

Janet M. Manuel (Isabela, Philippines)

The Light of the World

Read John 9:1–17

Jesus said, 'I am the light of the world. Whoever follows me will never walk in darkness, but will have the light of life.'

John 8:12 (NIV)

One of my favourite sayings is 'Let's shed some light on this'. It's a familiar expression to use when you want to take a closer look at an object or situation and examine it from a different angle.

The phrase came to mind recently when I noticed that vision is central to Jesus' ministry. All four Gospels include stories of Jesus healing people who were blind. In John's Gospel, Jesus heals a man blind from birth by making mud and rubbing it on his eyes. Instead of delighting in the miracle, the Pharisees challenge Jesus because he healed on a Sabbath. Jesus responds by saying again, 'I am the light of the world', but this time he adds a warning about spiritual blindness.

Jesus is asking all of us to open our eyes and see differently. He wants us to remove our blinkers and to look closely and lovingly at people and situations around us. Have we failed to see that a neighbour is struggling? Have we been second-guessing a colleague's motivations or are we frustrated by a church member's actions without realising we are the ones in the dark? Jesus encourages us to wipe away our spiritual blindness and gain a new vision. When we live in Christ, we can shed some light on the unexpected.

Prayer: *Dear Jesus, you are the light of the world. Remove our blinkers so we can see your truth. Help us to be a reflection of your light. Amen*

Thought for the day: Christ gives us new vision to spread his light to the world.

Sherry Elliott (Tennessee, US)

PRAYER FOCUS: THOSE WHO ARE SPIRITUALLY BLIND

A Light for Jesus

Read Matthew 5:13–16
Let your light shine before others, that they may see your good deeds and glorify your Father in heaven.
Matthew 5:16 (NIV)

'Oh! I'm sorry!' The old lady turned from tidying her car boot to see Keith holding a bag of compost. 'I didn't realise you were waiting with my purchase. I was just making room for the bags.'

Keith returned her smile. 'No problem.' He placed the bag of compost then returned for a second. 'I see by the sign of the fish on your window that you're a Christian,' he commented as he closed her boot.

The lady's smile disappeared. 'Yes,' she snapped, 'but I don't like to talk about it.'

Keith watched her drive off before returning to work and silently praying for the old lady.

As my friend later relayed the incident to me I felt a rush of sadness. Here were two Christians, one shining a light for Jesus, the other hiding her light under a bowl. As Christians we need to share Jesus with the world, using words and actions when opportunities arise, to be lights piercing the darkness.

Prayer: *Lord, help us to be generous with our faith and not keep it to ourselves. May your Spirit give us the courage to share with others. Blow upon our smoking coals and turn us into blazing beacons for you. Amen*

Thought for the day: Do I need to be reignited for God?

Julia Cutting (Yorkshire, England)

Zip Upside Down!

Read Jeremiah 17:7–8

Trust in the Lord with all your heart, and do not rely on your own insight.
Proverbs 3:5 (NRSV)

Recently my family and I went on a zip-line adventure. After climbing a 65-step tower, we zipped from tower to tower while holding one hand loosely on the zip line to control our speed. To steady us, we placed the other hand on the overhead cable that connected our seat harness to the zip line. On our final tower, our instructor told us we could zip upside down by folding our legs up close to our bodies and leaning back. I had really wanted to experience this, but regardless of how far I leaned back, I could not do it.

Later I realised that I could not because I had not trusted enough in myself to 'let go' of the overhead cable. I thought how true that is of life. To enjoy our life with God fully, we must 'let go'—let go of our old life with its worries, old habits and old ways of doing things. Then we will be free to enjoy the adventure of the abundant life God intends for us.

Prayer: *Dear Lord, help us to trust you not only in the big things in our lives but also the small, everyday things, as we pray, 'Our Father which art in heaven, Hallowed be thy name. Thy kingdom come. Thy will be done in earth, as it is in heaven. Give us this day our daily bread. And forgive us our debts, as we forgive our debtors. And lead us not into temptation, but deliver us from evil: For thine is the kingdom, and the power, and the glory, for ever.'* Amen*

Thought for the day: We can trust God to lead us to an abundant life (see John 10:10).

Phyllis W. Howard (Missouri, US)

Scars

Read Isaiah 53:1–5

He was pierced for our transgressions, he was crushed for our iniquities; the punishment that brought us peace was on him, and by his wounds we are healed.

Isaiah 53:5 (NIV)

When I first saw the video in an online, I winced. It featured a young woman in Vietnam with a scar etching an uneven path across her cheek. The scar bore witness that she had suffered at the hands of persecutors for her love of Jesus.

Then I noticed the earring, dangling from her ear just at the end of the scar. The golden cross was a sparkling testimony. 'My love endures,' God seemed to whisper. I doubt I would have noticed the cross had it not been for the scar.

What would happen if I allowed others to see the scars on my heart caused by past hurts and fears? Would they wince? Or would seeing my scars draw their attention to the cross? Could God use me to comfort others with the same comfort he had given me, as we read in 2 Corinthians 1:4?

We all have scars whether visible or invisible. Because God's love outshines my scars, I can help someone else—whether through a phone call, a soup kitchen or simply through lending a listening ear. Even when it means being honest about my own struggles, with God's help I can speak, listen and act with love.

Prayer: *Dear God, your scars led us to life. Please use ours to draw others to you. In Jesus' name. Amen*

Thought for the day: How can my scars lead others to Christ?

Bonnie Rose Hudson (Pennsylvania, US)

How to Pray

Read Psalm 138:1–3

The Lord's eyes are on the righteous and his ears are open to their prayers.
1 Peter 3:12 (CEB)

I was on the phone with my friend Jen the other day, discussing a particularly troubling dilemma she was experiencing. She was looking for advice, yet the only advice I could offer was that she should pray about her problem.

'Pray?' she asked. 'But how? There are so many prayers. Which one should I say?'

Through the years, I've turned to prayer in times of need and in times of gratitude, too. What I have discovered is that no one specific prayer or method of praying works better than another. As I told Jen, speaking a simple prayer like 'Help me, God,' in a hospital intensive care unit can be just as effective as reciting a psalm while on my knees in church.

God knows our hearts. What's important is that we speak to our Lord in the best way we can and then listen for the answer.

Prayer: *Dear Lord, how comforting it is to know that prayer, in any form, is powerful. Thank you for hearing the needs of our hearts. We pray in the name of Jesus. Amen*

Thought for the day: God hears—and answers—our prayers.

Monica A. Andermann (New York, US)

PRAYER FOCUS: THOSE WHO HAVE GIVEN UP ON PRAYER

Remembering what's Important

Read Deuteronomy 6:4–12

Simon Peter answered him: 'Lord, to whom can we go? You have the words of eternal life.'
John 6:68 (NRSV)

Our son is four years old. Recently we were at a parents' meeting at his nursery school. The English language teacher was complaining that the children have poor memories, that they forget the meanings of words, and said that we parents must help our children to practise this language.

Her comments made me worry about my son's education. But soon after, I heard my son recite the Apostles' Creed for the first time. He also knows the Lord's Prayer. As I listened, I realised that he has no problem with his memory.

Thank God that we live today in a prosperous time with so many opportunities and doors open to our children. We try to teach our children multiple languages from an early age as part of helping them in later life. But the Bible teaches us that even in these good times the most important thing is to remember the Lord (see Deuteronomy 6:6–9). More important than our children's learning the words which help them to live in the modern world is for them to be taught God's life-giving word.

Prayer: *Dear Lord, help us to learn your words and teach them to our children. Amen*

Thought for the day: How will I remember God's word today?

Fedor Kim (Moscow, Russia)

PRAYER FOCUS: CHILDREN WHO ARE NOT ABLE TO GO TO SCHOOL

Hidden Treasure

Read Isaiah 54:9–12

God demonstrates his own love for us in this: While we were still sinners, Christ died for us.

Romans 5:8 (NIV)

A heavy ceramic pot with a wooden cover sits on our patio. Recently, my husband was working outside and moved the pot out of the way. He heard something clatter, removed the cover and found an old tin can filled with stones. A note inside the can read 'To Dad, with love from Jenna.'

Our daughter, Jenna, is now 27 years old. When I told her what her father had found, she said she had no memory of writing the note or placing the can of stones inside the pot. But the handwriting was definitely hers. We wondered what had led her to hide her treasure in the pot. Whatever Jenna's reason, finding the treasure brought joy to my husband. He could picture Jenna searching for perfect stones and carefully writing the note to him. Her note was a sweet reminder of her love for him.

In a similar way, we can find sweet reminders in the Bible, treasures God has placed there for us. If we don't open our Bibles, we never find those treasures. But when we do and a verse speaks to us in a deep way, we know we have found a love note from our Father.

Prayer: *Holy Father, as we read your word, open our hearts so that we may know your love for us. Instil your words in our hearts so that we may share your treasure with others. Amen*

Thought for the day: God knows me and loves me.

Valerie A. Foster (New York, US)

Always With Us

Read John 10:11–18

Jesus said, 'I am the good shepherd. The good shepherd lays down his life for the sheep.'
John 10:11 (CEB)

I was in a meeting when it started. We all looked out the window in awe of the unfamiliar 'white stuff' falling from the sky. 'Wow! The forecasters were right!' exclaimed one of my colleagues. We abruptly headed to our cars so that we could get home before the snow got worse. But it was too late. The snowstorm caught us unprepared, crippling the city and its transport systems. People were stranded in cars, at work, at school and on buses. People abandoned their vehicles and walked miles in order to pick up their children or find a place that was warm and dry. Food and water became luxuries as getting to a shop or finding an open restaurant proved an almost impossible task.

As I sat in my car for hours, wondering if I would make it home, I started to become anxious. And then I remembered the promises of the good shepherd who knows each one of us by name and all of our needs. Because we have a good shepherd who knows us and sacrificed his life for us, we 'lack nothing' and we 'fear no danger'. Our Good Shepherd is always with us.

Prayer: *Dear God, thank you for being our good shepherd and staying with us at all times. Amen*

Thought for the day: The Lord is my good shepherd.

Jasmine Rose Smothers (Georgia, US)

The Other Son

Read Luke 15:25–32

'My son,' the father said, 'you are always with me, and everything I have is yours. But we had to celebrate and be glad, because this brother of yours was dead and is alive again; he was lost and is found.'
Luke 15:31–32 (NIV)

The story of the prodigal son is one of Jesus' most familiar parables. When we study the story, the relationship between the father and the son usually gets most of our attention. However, we sometimes forget the other son in the story—the older brother.

Remember when the younger brother came back home and his father threw a party to celebrate his return? The older brother refused to go. Instead, he spent his time pouting and complaining. Unfortunately, sometimes I can relate more to the older than to the younger brother. When I find it hard to rejoice when others rejoice or I complain when things do not go my way, I am acting like him. When I criticise the good efforts of others instead of focusing on God and pleasing him no matter what others do around me, I am acting just like that older brother. When I do not rejoice when others come back to a faithful walk with God, I am acting just like him.

At the end of today's story the father and the younger son were still rejoicing, and the older son was still grumbling. Instead of being resentful we can focus our attention on God, on sharing the gospel of Christ with others, and on welcoming all 'prodigals' on their way back to our Father.

Prayer: *Dear Father, keep us aware of our attitudes and actions that take us away from you. In Jesus' name we pray. Amen*

Thought for the day: Because God has welcomed me, I will welcome others.

Andy Baker (Tennessee, US)

Justice, Grace, Mercy

Read Matthew 7:1–5

Do not judge, so that you may not be judged.
Matthew 7:1 (NRSV)

Recently, someone treated me unfairly. I had to deal with the hurt and anger I felt toward the other person. I wanted justice. Then, as God's Spirit started to work in me, I realised that my attitude was not pleasing to God. I stopped, prayed and asked for his wisdom.

God responded with a question, 'How have I dealt with you when you acted inappropriately toward another person?' I knew the answer immediately: he has treated me with grace and mercy. My Saviour, Jesus Christ, who went to the cross on my behalf, received the justice I deserve. God also helps me to realise that the other person's treatment of me was a once-only event, compared to the many times I was treated with dignity and respect. What occurred could have happened to anyone for many reasons and was probably not a personal affront.

I realised that I should deal with the situation and the other person with grace and mercy, leaving justice in God's hands. I asked his forgiveness for being rash, and my spirit returned to a state of peace. My goal is to be like Christ, so I need to treat others as the Lord treats me.

Prayer: *Dear Lord, help us to treat others with the grace and mercy you show to us through Jesus Christ. Amen*

Thought for the day: Am I showing God's grace to those around me?

Jose G. Chavez (Mississippi, US)

Being Grafted

Read Romans 11:16–24

You, though a wild olive shoot, have been grafted in among the others and now share in the nourishing sap from the olive root.
Romans 11:17 (NIV)

Once, my father grafted a pear-tree branch into an apple tree. First he cut a thick branch off our apple tree, creating a flat surface on the trunk. Then he cut a slit on the flat surface and placed the pear branch in the slit. Finally, he covered it with tar, so the graft could attach to the apple tree. In time, the grafted branch produced fruit that looked like an apple but tasted like a pear.

After seeing this process, I understood the Romans 11 verse much better. When we come to salvation, the Lord cuts us off from our old way of life and grafts us into the family of God. Jesus' dying on the cross opened the door for us to be adopted into the new family. We receive the seal of the Holy Spirit. We are also added to Christ's Church (see Acts 2:47)—a spiritual family that will provide for us the nurture, fellowship and accountability essential for healthy growth and fruitfulness.

Each of us needs to belong to a community of faith. If we are a new believer or someone new to a particular church congregation, we may find it difficult to feel connected and established. However, the Lord will graft us into a church family if we stay patient with the process. As we grow, we will produce love, joy, patience, and other fruit of the Spirit (see Galatians 5:22).

Prayer: *Redeeming God, help us to grow as we are established in a church family. Amen*

Thought for the day: Through Jesus we have been grafted into God's family.

Karline Fischer (California, US)

PRAYER FOCUS: THOSE VISITING A NEW CHURCH

Strength through Obedience

Read John 14:15–27

Jesus [said], 'Those who love me will keep my word, and my Father will love them, and we will come to them and make our home with them.'
John 14:23 (NRSV)

My wife, Berta, had been paralysed for two decades and was now in hospital with pneumonia. Our minister called to encourage us and commended me for the way I had cared for my wife since the accident that led to her paralysis.

I appreciated his attempt to support us. But, tired as I was, I was more direct than usual. 'Don't praise me for not breaking my word. I'm only keeping the promise I made when we married.' That day we had promised God, our minister and the church that we would care for each other 'in sickness and in health… so long as [we] both shall live'.

I explained that the thing that makes my actions possible is the certainty that I am doing the will of God. After all, how often do we actually have that certainty?

Being a long-term carer is certainly difficult. I don't always do it as well as I should, and I require constant help from God and his people. But in this matter I am doing the will of God.

I have discovered that loving Jesus and obeying Jesus are two sides of the same coin. And in my experience, when God calls us to do something, he gives us the ability to obey.

Prayer: *O God, thank you for working through us so that we may be as Christ to others. Amen*

Thought for the day: There is tremendous power in obeying God.

Earl Dickerson (Kentucky, US)

Five Little Tomatoes

Read Matthew 3:13–17

[Jesus] said to [his disciples], 'But who do you say that I am?'
Matthew 16:15 (NRSV)

I was preserving vegetables, carefully filling jars with little cherry tomatoes. Five tomatoes remained in the bowl. My four-year-old son was attentively following the process and commented: 'This,' he said, pointing at the ones in the bowl, 'looks like a smile!' Moving to look from the other side, he said, 'And now it's a rainbow!' Then smiling mischievously, my son quickly grabbed all the tomatoes and stuffed them into his mouth. Laughing and raising my eyebrows, I asked: 'And what is it now?' 'Vitamins!' he said.

This interchange reminded me of how important it is to try to see the world from different perspectives. We humans often only look at the obvious, but God has a different perspective. After all, Jesus did not just see a tax collector in Zacchaeus. In the woman who wiped his feet with her hair, everyone saw only a sinner but the Lord saw differently. And even in Jesus himself many saw one of the prophets, but God called Jesus 'my Son, the Beloved' (Matthew 3:17). As people of faith, we can strive to see the world from God's perspective.

Prayer: *Dear God, open our eyes that we may see the world from your perspective. Amen*

Thought for the day: Who am I in God's eyes?

Natalya Ilyushonok (Hrodna, Belarus)

The Value of Questions

Read 1 Peter 1:3–9

Peter, however, got up and ran to the tomb… He saw the strips of linen lying by themselves, and he went away, wondering to himself what had happened.

Luke 24:12 (NIV)

'Why is this? Why is that?' My small son bombarded me with questions about everything he could see on the way to the shops, finally asking amusingly, 'Why do I keep asking why?' He was learning by asking questions and listening to the answers, and continued to do so until he grew older. Now it's his turn to answer his children's never-ending questions.

On resurrection morning, Peter did the same thing. He rushed to investigate as soon as he heard the women tell of all they had seen and heard. He went right into the tomb and found it empty except for the strips of linen lying there, and it had a profound impact on him. Now he needed answers to his questions, for this was something completely outside his experience or expectations.

In the letter Peter wrote to other believers much later, we see the faith-building answers he had found and how he passed them on in his vibrant testimony: 'Praise be to the God and Father of our Lord Jesus Christ! In his great mercy he has given us new birth into a living hope' (1 Peter 1:3).

We all have puzzling questions. But in the Bible and in prayer we can ask God to open our eyes to see, our minds to understand and our spirits to believe.

Prayer: *Eternal God, help us to look into your word to find answers to our questions, so that we grow in faith and in understanding. Amen*

Thought for the day: Jesus promised that when we ask, seek and knock, we will find.

Hazel V. Thompson (Somerset, England)

Clinging to Christ

Read John 15:1–9

Jesus said, 'I am the vine; you are the branches.'
John 15:5 (CEB)

I first noticed the little branch after a night of harsh storm. Bent down in an awkward position, it caught my eye during morning prayer as I looked out of my bedroom window. Other branches reached out and up toward the sky, strong and unscathed. But this one slender branch dangled toward the ground—damaged but not detached from the tree.

I was surprised to see this little bent-down branch still hanging there the next morning. I had expected it to drop to the ground, but there it was—still dangling and vulnerable. The same was true the next day and the next. Watching this damaged branch became part of my morning prayer for the season of Lent. No matter how stormy it was, the branch clung to the life-source of the tree.

How like that branch I often am—bent down and vulnerable to the storms of life. And like the branch, I cling to Christ, my life-source, trusting that even when I am 'hanging on by a thread' Christ will cling to me as well. My wounded, fragile and awkward self will always be connected to Christ. Jesus says, 'I am the vine; you are the branches. If you remain in me and I in you, then you will produce much fruit. Without me, you can't do anything' (John 15:5). In Christ there is life that holds on to and remains in us at all times.

Prayer: *Dear God, help us to cling to you throughout life's storms. Thank you for the peace you offer us. Amen*

Thought for the day: Jesus' presence sustains and strengthens us.

Pamela Hawkins (Tennessee, US)

Aware of God's Timing

Read Matthew 7:7–11
Ask and it will be given to you; seek and you will find.
Matthew 7:7 (NIV)

I recently retired after 51 years in ministry, and I was struggling with how to be useful. One morning in my prayer time, I asked God to show me how I could be of service both to him and others that day.

A few hours later I was driving through a local shopping centre when I noticed a mobile blood-donor vehicle and a sign asking for blood donors. As a long-time donor, I thought that was something I could do; I would have to do that one day. Then that inner voice that the Holy Spirit uses to get our attention reminded me that I had asked God to give me something to do today. So I walked over to the vehicle and signed up to donate then and there.

That experience reminded me that when we ask God for direction for our lives, we need to look and listen for the answers that he gives. Otherwise, we may miss the very moment we prayed for.

Prayer: *Gracious God, who listens to all our prayers, give us eyes to see and ears to hear your answers—and a willing spirit to respond. As Jesus taught us, we pray, 'Our Father in heaven, hallowed be your name, your kingdom come, your will be done, on earth as it is in heaven. Give us today our daily bread. And forgive us our debts, as we also have forgiven our debtors. And lead us not into temptation, but deliver us from the evil one.'* Amen*

Thought for the day: God's timing is perfect.

Richard N. Ryley (New York, US)

The Old Pink Chair

Read 2 Timothy 1:3–14

I am reminded of your sincere faith, a faith that lived first in your grandmother Lois and your mother Eunice and now, I am sure, lives in you.

2 Timothy 1:5 (NRSV)

My mother struggled with drug addiction throughout her life. I was brought up by my grandmother. She took me to Sunday school and church, and she held on to the hope that I would become a pastor. In my youth, I made bad choices that put me on the path of drugs, gangs and crime. Every morning, my grandmother sat in her old pink chair, reading her Bible and her copy of *The Upper Room*. On some mornings, I was just coming in from the night before. She sat up entire nights waiting, worrying and praying for my safe return. She never gave up hope for me.

Ultimately, through my grandmother's love and witness, I found Christ and became a pastor. A couple of years ago, my teenage daughter decided she would run away. I found myself powerless and sick with worry. I discovered that I too have 'an old pink chair'; I sat reading my Bible and *The Upper Room*, praying for my daughter's safe return. She did return home, and today she seems to be inheriting the faith that I learned from my grandmother. I will never forget my grandmother's old pink chair and the great faith it represented.

Prayer: *Dear God, help us to live our faith in such a way that our children will see and believe. Thank you for the witness of those who have gone before us. Amen*

Thought for the day: Are we living a legacy of faith for our children?

Michael A. Beck (Florida, US)

An Unlikely Offering

Read Psalm 142:1–7

I pour out before him my complaint; before him I tell my trouble.
Psalm 142:2 (NIV)

One day while at work, I was worrying about some health problems I was facing. Angry about these problems, I realised that I had been complaining. I considered giving these concerns to God but then had second thoughts. Several Bible verses make it plain that God doesn't want to listen to a complaining spirit (see Numbers 11:1, Philippians 2:14 and 1 Peter 4:9). However, I started unloading my concerns to him anyway. No one else was there to hear my complaints and I needed help.

Then a strange thing happened. I had expected to feel God's displeasure but instead I felt peace. The tension I had experienced just a few minutes before had disappeared. I felt God was pleased, not with my complaining but with my willingness to trust him enough to express even the unpleasant things in my life.

Before this experience, I thought of an 'offering' as money I put into a collection plate at church. That particular day at work the only 'offering' I had to give to God wasn't pleasant. But God—in grace, mercy and compassion—accepted it and showed me that my offerings of trust are valued.

Prayer: *O God, we thank you that in trusting you with the difficult things in our lives we find peace, hope and healing. Amen*

Thought for the day: God wants to hear the good and bad of our lives.

Peggy Booher (Pennsylvania, US)

Our Father's Strength

Read Job 42:1–6

Job replied to the Lord: 'I know that you can do all things; no purpose of yours can be thwarted.'

Job 42:1–2 (NIV)

From the time I was five, wrestling with my dad was our ritual. He'd pin me down; sometimes he let me win. As I grew, the struggles got more intense. When I was 13 I beat him, and I could tell that he had used all of his strength. I was elated—for about 30 seconds. As Dad walked quietly away, a feeling of sadness washed over me. I'm stronger than my dad, I thought. That's not supposed to happen. If Dad's not stronger than me, how can he be my authority and my protector?

Since the garden of Eden, we've yearned to be smarter than God. In his desperation, Job came to that point (see Job 10). Job didn't want to be greater than God, any more than I wanted actually to be stronger than my dad. If I was stronger than Dad, then it seemed to me that my 13-year-old's strength was all I had to rely on. Job wanted God to be his ultimate resource with the assurance that he was God's child. 'Before, you were only a theory to me,' Job was saying. 'Now, I know that you are my ultimate reality.'

How reassuring it is to discover that our salvation does not lie in our own cleverness and strength! God's power is a loving power in which we, like Job, become free to experience a peace and comfort that only God can give.

Prayer: *O God, help us to remember that our achievements matter only when your power resides in us. Amen*

Thought for the day: When we acknowledge God's power, we can experience peace.

George A. Nye (Oregon, US)

Things I Take for Granted

Read John 15:10–21

Pray for us that the message of the Lord may spread rapidly and be honoured.

2 Thessalonians 3:1 (NIV)

I sat in my cosy chair and read my Bible. Then I scanned Facebook. My attention was captured by a memorial to William Tyndale carved with a statement that Tyndale was convicted of heresy and, on 6 October 1536, was executed for translating the Bible into English.

This memorial made me think of how often I take things for granted. I have freedom to attend church, to read my Bible and to share my beliefs. My family honours God and supports my faith. I don't have much money, but I'm rich in freedom. Jesus died to save me from my sin. Soldiers died defending my freedoms. William Tyndale died so I can read the Bible in English. While I enjoy these privileges, some people today face rejection and death threats from their own families for following Jesus Christ. Others are persecuted, imprisoned or killed for their faith.

Knowing all this, I now pick up my Bible with renewed reverence. I sing with a grateful heart and pray for fellow believers in other countries who are suffering for their faith.

Prayer: *Dear Lord Jesus, thank you for the gifts of salvation, the Bible and freedom. Be with our brothers and sisters who are suffering for you. Amen*

Thought for the day: We have freedom to pursue our faith today because of choices people made yesterday.

Ruth L. Snyder (Alberta, Canada)

Jesus Has Arrived!

Read Matthew 21:1–11
I will tell of your name to my brothers and sisters; in the midst of the congregation I will praise you.
Psalm 22:22 (NRSV)

On Palm Sunday 1997, I stood at the church pulpit and held my testimony in shaking hands, silently asking Jesus to grant me the courage to read it. I shared with the congregation that my brother's death the year before had forced me to evaluate my life. I told them how meaningless and purposeless my life had felt. I said that even though I had not attended a church in many years, I had sensed God guiding me to theirs, so I had called to speak with their pastor.

Whenever I glanced at the congregation, I was nervous. To calm myself I focused on the palm fronds they held to commemorate the day when crowds proclaimed Jesus' triumphant arrival by spreading branches on the road into Jerusalem. When I shared my testimony that Palm Sunday, I was proclaiming the arrival of Jesus into my heart. I told the congregation that their pastor had led me to Jesus and that the gift of salvation brings hope and healing. I asserted that serving in God's kingdom brings purpose and peace. On this Palm Sunday, we all can celebrate and proclaim the day Jesus entered *our* lives.

Prayer: *Dear Lord Jesus Christ, give us the boldness and joy to proclaim your glorious gift of salvation. Amen*

Thought for the day: Jesus is still making triumphant arrivals.

Debra Pierce (Massachusetts, US)

PRAYER FOCUS: SOMEONE SHARING THEIR TESTIMONY   97

Jesus is the Way

Read John 13:36—14:6

Jesus answered, 'I am the way and the truth and the life.'
John 14:6 (NIV)

Once I asked a young man for directions to a place in an unfamiliar city. Instead of giving me directions, he offered to go with me. He not only showed the way; he became the way! I just had to follow him. Thomas asks Jesus, 'How can we know the way?' Rather than giving directions, Jesus answers 'I am the Way.' He becomes the way and Thomas simply has to follow him.

What does it mean to accept Jesus as my way and follow him? In John 13:36 Simon Peter asks Jesus, 'Lord, where are you going?' The conversation that follows clearly shows that Jesus is actually talking about the way of the cross—the offering of his life in self-sacrificial love. It is the way of laying down one's life for one's friends (see John 15:13). When Jesus says, 'No one comes to the Father except through me', he is talking about *how* one comes to God. Jesus teaches us that there is no way to reach the heart of God, except through self-sacrificial and unconditional love.

Early Christians were known as those who belonged to the Way (see Acts 9:2). If Jesus is our Way, then we will walk with Jesus today and love our neighbours with an unconditional and self-sacrificial love.

Prayer: *Loving God, give us hearts to love you and to love others unconditionally. Amen*

Thought for the day: Jesus shows us the way.

M. Thomas Thangaraj (Massachusetts, US)

Not a Hummingbird?

Read Psalm 139:13–16 and Romans 12:3–8

I praise you because I am fearfully and wonderfully made; your works are wonderful, I know that full well.

Psalm 139:14 (NIV)

A beautiful purple finch was trying desperately to drink from our hummingbird feeder. Watching it furiously flap its wings in an attempt to maintain an airborne drinking position, I said, 'Don't you know you're not a hummingbird?' Eventually the finch hurried to secure footing on a nearby tree branch. It seemed to have realised that it could not hover like a hummingbird.

Observing this finch caused me to ask myself, 'How often do I attempt, or wish to be, something or somebody I am not?' No matter how much I have wished I had the wood-carving talent of my two brothers or my wife's ability to play the piano by ear, I have come to realise that these abilities are not mine. That is not the way my Creator put me together. But God has given me some talents that neither my brothers nor my wife have. In divine wisdom and grace, God made us each different.

When we realise that God has created each of us as unique individuals, we can confidently live as the people he created us to be. This means we can celebrate our personal uniqueness and search for special ways that we may share that uniqueness with family, community and church. Such celebrating and sharing can be a tangible way for us to praise and thank God for creating us the way we are.

Prayer: *Marvellous Creator, help us to celebrate our uniqueness and to use it to make a positive difference in the lives of others. Amen*

Thought for the day: Our uniqueness is a living example of God's boundless grace.

Roger Wayne Hicks (Arizona, US)

Renovations

Read Galatians 5:22–25

O Lord, you are our Father; we are the clay, and you are our potter; we are all the work of your hand.
Isaiah 64:8 (NRSV)

My daughter-in-law walked past some old houses that were being renovated. She told me how chaotic they looked during the process and wondered how they would look when they were finished. She was keen to see the renovations completed—the final result of all the builders' hard work.

This conversation reminded me of our spiritual renovation process through the work of the Holy Spirit in us. As the Spirit works in our lives, God brings to the surface areas that need healing, attitudes that need changing, sins that need repentance and relationships that need restoring.

Like the house renovations, the process can be messy and sometimes painful. However, God deals with us lovingly and gently. He is the Master Builder with perfect timing. We are works in progress, and we become more like Jesus during our spiritual transformation.

When we lean on God and persevere, he will transform and sanctify us. How exciting it is to know that God is in the process of renovating us so that we are becoming the children we were created to be.

Prayer: *Heavenly Father, thank you for the work of your Holy Spirit in us. May we reach our full potential as your children and serve you well and with joy. Amen*

Thought for the day: Today I will strive to be all that God wants me to be.

Ann Stewart (South Australia, Australia)

This Changes Everything

Read John 14:15–21, 27

God so loved the world that he gave his one and only Son, that whoever believes in him shall not perish but have eternal life.
John 3:16 (NIV)

I had been diagnosed with a rare cancer. On Easter morning, we clung to each other in church, especially moved by our pastor's proclamation, 'Jesus died for our sins, and today he has risen and is alive. He conquered death so that we can live eternally in heaven with our merciful God. This, friends, changes everything.'

As we let the pastor's words sink in, my husband and I exchanged a glance. Our minds were whirling with the news of my cancer and with the task of telling our children. In the past, I would have spun out of control with worry. Twelve years ago, I invited Jesus Christ to be Lord of my life. I trust him not only with my cancer but with every breath I take and with my salvation when I leave this world.

Knowing that life is preparation for eternity and realising that I am forgiven and will spend eternity with God gives me security and peace. Jesus said, 'In this world you will have trouble. But take heart! I have overcome the world' (John 16:33). This, friends, changes everything. Because I feel Jesus' constant love and presence, I can cope with my diagnosis, praying constantly, instead of worrying.

Prayer: *Loving God, increase our faith, fill our hearts with your peace, and help us to trust you in all the circumstances of our lives. Amen*

Thought for the day: The promise of Easter changes everything.

Kathleen Buskirk (California, US)

Towel Mentality

Read John 13:1–17

Jesus said, 'Now that I, your Lord and Teacher, have washed your feet, you also should wash one another's feet.'
John 13:14 (NIV)

Recently, I realised that what keeps me spiritually grounded is serving other people. When I face tough times in my own life or when I have more questions than answers, I want to 'take up a towel' as Jesus demonstrated in John 13. Jesus was facing crucifixion. But instead of taking up arms or calling twelve legions of angels (see Matthew 26:53), Jesus wrapped a towel around his waist and started washing his disciples' feet.

When we face trials, it's easy to focus on only our own problems. While we wait on the Lord to answer our prayers or while we search for answers, we often become impatient and ask God when, why or how? Instead, we could simply search for opportunities to serve and bless others. When we take on a 'towel mentality' and humble ourselves, we become the hands and feet of Christ.

Prayer: *Dear God, develop in us a servant's heart. Help us to be sensitive to the many ways we can serve others at home, work, school and church. Amen*

Thought for the day: To whom can I serve as Christ's hands and feet today?

Brad Richardson (Georgia, US)

Finding Joy

Read John 16:20–27

For the joy set before him [Jesus] endured the cross, scorning its shame, and sat down at the right hand of the throne of God.
Hebrews 12:2 (NIV)

Like many other people, I live with pain. My pain is physical because of the early onset of arthritis. But I have known others whose pain is mental, emotional or spiritual in nature, and their hurt is often greater than bodily pain.

Jesus endured the suffering of the cross, which included every type of pain. He suffered obvious physical pain; but along with that came the sorrow and grief of leaving his disciples, the shame of public humiliation and the feeling of rejection by his Father as he hung on the cross. Yet Jesus was able to look ahead to the joy that was to come.

The use of the word 'joy' is amazing to me. Joy goes beyond the relief of pain; in fact, it seems to be the very opposite of pain. The definition of joy includes feelings of happiness, gladness and delight.

Faith calls us to look beyond our pain to a time when our health, happiness, and even our joy can be restored. Jesus Christ is always our example and guide for overcoming the difficulties of life, especially when we are hurting.

Prayer: *Dear Lord, be with us in our difficult times. May we abide in your presence, where we can always find joy. Amen*

Thought for the day: Joy comes from trusting God's love for us.

Lois M. Baker (Arkansas, US)

PRAYER FOCUS: SOMEONE LIVING WITH CHRONIC PAIN   103

The Day After

Read Luke 23:26–56

The [angels] said… 'Why do you look for the living among the dead? He is not here, but has risen.'
Luke 24:5 (NRSV)

Friday was a bad day. The sky turned dark in the middle of the afternoon as a devastating tornado approached. Once the storm had passed, a mass of broken glass, bricks, trees and twisted steel remained. The day that followed the storm in Mississippi left many people wondering where they would live, how they would recover from their losses, where they would work and how life would go on.

The Friday described in Luke 23 was also a bad day. Jesus had been arrested and sentenced to execution on the cross. As the day progressed, it got worse. Jesus was led outside the city, nailed to a cross and left to die. Late that day, his followers were allowed to claim the body and place it in a tomb. The day that followed Jesus' death was also a day of confusion and uncertainty. Many people had attached their hope and expectation to Jesus. And now that hope was dashed. In the eyes of the early believers, all was lost.

Too often in the aftermath of tragedy we lose our faith and embrace despair. We forget the promises in the Bible and the words of Jesus. We see no answers to our situation. In these times, we can remember that a new day is coming, just as it did that very first Easter morning.

Prayer: *O God, help us to recognise that Christ is standing with us as we go through dark days. Amen*

Thought for the day: Easter morning promises that dark days do not last for ever.

B.J. Woods (Texas, US)

Resurrection and Life

Read John 11:17–26

Jesus said to [Martha], 'I am the resurrection and the life. Those who believe in me, even though they die, will live, and everyone who lives and believes in me will never die.'

John 11:25–26 (NRSV)

When Jesus brought Lazarus back to life, he knew Lazarus would one day have to die again. What Jesus did was more like resuscitation. Resuscitation means restoring life back to the way it was. We want God to bring a loved one back, repair a relationship or return a job. We pray: 'God, just restore my life to the way it used to be.' Yet, the dialogue between Jesus and Lazarus' sisters reveals that this is a story for those who have to live with death. To them Jesus promises resurrection. There is a difference.

A friend of mine told me about an experience he had seven months after his wife died from cancer. He sensed God wanting to give him peace, but he was resistant. He wanted his wife back. How could he have peace? Several months later he felt God telling him, 'It's okay to have peace.' He lowered his resistance and soon found new possibilities emerging. He said, 'As long as I resisted, I couldn't discover the new possibilities God had for me.'

It's easy to crave resuscitation—to want God to return life to the way it was before, but Jesus said, 'I am the resurrection and the life.' He doesn't just restore. He transforms. Death can take away, but God gives new life. Christ is resurrection and life!

Prayer: *Living God, thank you for the gift of resurrection. Help us to embrace the new life you offer us. Amen*

Thought for the day: God offers us new life each day.

Rob Fuquay (Indiana, US)

Spotting God

Read James 1:19–25

Seek first [God's] kingdom and his righteousness, and all these things will be given to you as well.
Matthew 6:33 (NIV)

When I was a young child, I couldn't dance gracefully during spinning moves because I was worried about how I looked. My instructor reminded me repeatedly to look at the spot painted on the wall to help my balance. But I feared that if I took my eyes off the mirror for even a second, I would look foolish. One day, I finally took my teacher's advice. I forced my eyes away from the mirror and back to the spot on the wall. The change was instantaneous. I focused on the pattern—turn, spot, turn, spot—and I could dance!

Sometimes as Christians, we focus more on how we look than on where God wants us to look. But the Bible reminds us to look at God first. Matthew 6:33 says that if we do, then 'all these things will be given to you as well'. If we keep turning our focus back to God and his advice in scripture about how we are supposed to act, then we won't spin out of control.

Prayer: *Heavenly Father, please guide our steps and help us to keep our eyes focused on you and the way you want us to live. We pray as Jesus taught us, saying, 'Our Father which art in heaven, Hallowed be thy name. Thy kingdom come. Thy will be done, as in heaven, so in earth. Give us day by day our daily bread. And forgive us our sins; for we also forgive every one that is indebted to us. And lead us not into temptation; but deliver us from evil.'* Amen*

Thought for the day: Focusing on Jesus will help us keep a balanced life.

Kate Miller (Texas, US)

Extraordinary Effort

Read Genesis 32:22–32

Jacob said [to the angel of God], 'I will not let you go, unless you bless me.'

Genesis 32:26 (NRSV)

In my second year in veterinary college, one of my courses was a particular branch of anatomy. But because there was such a large amount of course work, I was not able to devote the study time that the anatomy class required. As the day for exams drew nearer, I became desperate. For four days, I immersed myself in thorough study. I felt as if my brain was steaming in a hot oven, but I learned what I needed to pass the exam. God often works through our desperation, calling us to put forth extraordinary effort to respond to the urgencies of the moment.

Jacob also became desperate for a new and better life. After putting forth extraordinary effort to wrestle with an angel of the Lord one night, Jacob cried out in desperation, 'I will not let you go, unless you bless me!'

People who put forth extraordinary efforts often get results. God wants us to put forth extraordinary efforts to bring about the dreams he has for us: to start on a new career path, to help people in need or to work in a local church. Maybe it's time for us to say with Jacob, 'I will not let you go, unless you bless me!'

Prayer: *Dear Lord, help us to be desperate enough to fulfil the purpose you have for us. Bless us, Lord, with courage and determination. Amen*

Thought for the day: Fulfilling God's dreams for us requires our extraordinary effort.

Nwakuche Emeka (Imo, Nigeria)

Stop, Breathe and Pray

Read James 3:3–12

The tongue is a small part of the body, but it makes great boasts. Consider what a great forest is set on fire by a small spark.
James 3:5 (NIV)

Recently, in a phone conversation with my sister, idle chatter about one thing led to another, and before long our conversation was filled with derogatory remarks and comments about other people. It seemed harmless but later I noticed that my energy had been sapped.

I knew that gossiping was wrong so I phoned my sister and asked her forgiveness for letting the conversation become so negative. She confessed to feeling the same way. She suggested that from now on we try to be more aware in our conversations. 'Stop, breathe and pray,' I suggested. We agreed that we had let one careless comment ignite another until we were ablaze with self-righteous indignation.

Though we have done better, we still slip up and need to remind each other to stop and think about the direction our conversation is going. We understand that speaking negatively not only affects our relationship with God and others but also has a detrimental effect on our spirits. Though they may seem insignificant, unkind words can spark into a raging inferno. Better to keep the fire from starting in the first place.

Prayer: *Gracious God, with your help, may our words be pleasant, sweet and healing. Amen*

Thought for the day: We honour God when—instead of gossiping—we stop, breathe and pray.

Deanna Baird (Michigan, US)

Strength in Words

Read Hebrews 1:1–8

I can do all things through him who strengthens me.
Philippians 4:13 (NRSV)

I was in my first year of college with two young children to care for. My husband and I were divorcing, and my grandmother had just died—all a few weeks before Christmas. As I began scraping up the funds to attend her funeral 2000 miles away, I also had to find someone to care for my children in my absence and deal with end-of-term exams. All these challenges didn't leave much room for grieving.

Later, my mother told me about her last visit to my grandmother. As Grandmother lay in the hospital bed, Mum told her about my struggles as a newly-single parent, trying to finish college. In Grandmother's response were simple words that have since carried me through many years of challenges. 'Tell her not to worry, because she's strong like me.' I'd never thought of myself as strong before then. I was just trying to survive each day.

It's amazing what words can do. Some tend to wound and weaken us, while others encourage, strengthen and uplift us. I am grateful for the words of our heavenly Father in scripture that can strengthen us daily, regardless of circumstances. God's words are loving and powerful. They never change and we can carry them forever in our hearts and minds.

Prayer: *Dear Lord, please never let us forget that whatever we are going through, we can be strong in you. Amen*

Thought for the day: God's word can change our lives.

Carlitta Cole-Kelly (California, US)

My Friend

Read Psalm 139:1–12

Jesus said, 'Remember, I am with you always, to the end of the age.'
Matthew 28:20 (NRSV)

It seemed as if everyone had siblings except me. Behind every door in the block of flats where I grew up were brothers and sisters. But they were not mine. Admittedly, I had a lot of friends. But something was missing: someone else, another.

When I was a child, I created my own imaginary friend. He had no name, but he was always there and we were very close. He slept under my bed. We liked the same food and the same kind of music. If our family went on holiday, he sat beside me in the back seat. When I started school, he was there. We could talk about everything. We laughed at the same things, and we cried together.

Eventually, I realised that my constant friend was not imaginary at all. It was Jesus who had moved into my childhood, and remained my faithful companion. Now I'm an adult. And fortunately for me, I'm still just as close to my friend.

My path has not always been straightforward and simple. But never, even for a moment, did I doubt his presence, his patience, his openness and love. In and through Jesus I have many friends. But above all, Jesus has opened doors to sisters and brothers I did not know existed. Millions of them.

Prayer: *Dear Jesus, we thank you for your life, your closeness and your grace that lead us each day. Amen*

Thought for the day: What a friend we have in Jesus!

Thomas Boström (Gotland, Sweden)

Received as Partners

Read Philemon 1:1–25

If you consider me your partner, welcome [Onesimus] as you would welcome me.

Philemon v. 17 (NRSV)

Recently, *Saat Teduh* (the Indonesian edition of *The Upper Room*) readers' fellowship went to a prison to worship with the inmates. I imagined the prison to be a godless place. But when we got there, we discovered something amazing—a well-organised church. They have a good place for worship, talented musicians and even gifted choirs. They offered us a warm welcome. They read *The Upper Room* every day, and their spirituality is growing. And even though they live behind prison walls, they have freedom in Christ. I am excited to know that they are our partners in prayer.

In the apostle Paul's letter to Philemon we learn that people can change. Whether at home, in the office or even in a prison, the place does not matter. Just as Onesimus' faith allowed him to serve others, I believe that our friends in the prisons can also serve in God's kingdom. As part of God's family they join us in the chain of prayers around the globe.

Prayer: *Dear Lord, thank you for our partners in Christ. Teach us to be more devoted to you. Help us to be a blessing wherever we are. Amen*

Thought for the day: We are all partners in prayer.

Daniel Budiantoro (Jakarta, Indonesia)

I Am Mephibosheth

Read 2 Samuel 9:1–13

Encourage one another and build each other up.
1 Thessalonians 5:11 (NIV)

After Jonathan died, David sought to show kindness to every member of Jonathan's family. Thus, for the rest of his life he provided care for Jonathan's son, Mephibosheth, who was lame.

In some ways, I am Mephibosheth. After being run over by a truck, I underwent 18 operations, including amputation of all my toes. And like Mephibosheth, I was graced by a king with unmerited favour. God, our king, showed himself to me through Christians of a nearby church. During my six-month hospital stay, they visited me daily and prayed for me.

Unlike Mephibosheth, however, I eventually walked again. But at first, I was so weak that besides providing me with transport to church, various members had to carry me into the building. Until I regained strength, their kind arms supported me.

Having Mephibosheth-like need, I had received David-like kindness. And now, with the Holy Spirit within me, I consider it a blessing to visit people in the hospital. I now understand that such kindness is an intrinsic part of a covenant with God, part of a pledge to share this saving grace.

Prayer: *Dear God, by your love's strength, may we be willing to extend your arms of never-ending grace. Amen*

Thought for the day: When we receive God's grace, we can extend it to others as well.

Vanessa Bruce Ingold (California, US)

True Treasures

Read Luke 15:4–10

The Lord said to Moses, 'If you faithfully obey me and stay true to my covenant, you will be my most precious possession out of all the peoples, since the whole earth belongs to me.'

Exodus 19:5 (CEB)

Growing up, I often retreated to my mother's bedroom and made a beeline for her jewellery box. Inside was the jewellery my mother had accumulated over the years. I loved counting the figures on her silver charm bracelet and hearing the jingle of her earrings when I shook them. I knew she valued her jewellery because of the care she took to keep it safe.

My mother knew where every ring and pearl necklace was placed. If one went missing, she scoured our home until she found it. She often reminded me, 'Hannah, as you collect special things, remember to treat them like the treasures they are.' I have taken her words to heart. I also have a wooden box filled with cherished jewellery and trinkets I want to keep safe.

Sometimes we forget that God views us as special treasures. When I struggle to feel beautiful or valued, I think of my mother's jewellery box and realise that God sees me as a precious jewel to be protected and loved. He sacrificed his Son to purchase us, and he treasures each one of us.

Prayer: *Gracious God, you know everything about us. In your eyes, we are 'fearfully and wonderfully made' (Psalm 139:14, NIV). Help us to see one another through your loving eyes and to accept the value and love you invest in us. Amen*

Thought for the day: God treasures us so that we can treasure others.

Hannah Covington (Illinois, US)

More than a Sandwich

Read James 2:14–18

Suppose a brother or a sister is without clothes and daily food. If one of you says to them, 'Go in peace; keep warm and well fed,' but does nothing about their physical needs, what good is it?
James 2:15–16 (NIV)

When I was 25 years old, I decided to travel to Ireland for a holiday. I met some other young adults in a hostel, and one night three of us were walking down a street in Dublin when a dishevelled-looking man and woman approached us asking for money to buy food. Despite the objections of one of our party, we gave them some money. As the couple walked away, the person who had objected told us that he suspected they would use the money for drugs or alcohol. He then announced that he was going to follow them to prove it!

Somewhat unwillingly, my other companion and I went along. We followed the couple across the River Liffey down a street where raucous laughter filled the air as people drifted in and out of the many pubs. Just as my friend began to say, 'I told you so', the couple appeared, coming out of a supermarket with two sandwiches. In silence, we all looked at one another and realised that the sandwiches weren't the most important gifts given that day. The gift we had received was a reminder that we are not called to judge human hearts. We are simply called to emulate Jesus by responding with compassion to the human needs we encounter.

Prayer: *Dear Jesus, help us to be like you by responding to human needs with compassion rather than judgement. Amen*

Thought for the day: God calls us to show compassion, not judgement.

Wade Griffith (Alabama, US)

The Prodigal Daughter

Read Luke 15:11–24

The father said, 'This son of mine was dead and is alive again; he was lost and is found!'
Luke 15:24 (NRSV)

I started my journey with everything I owned packed inside my small car, even though the idea of leaving my flat, job, friends and my comfortable life of sin had paralysed me. The drive home seemed like a lifetime; I dreaded returning to face my mum. Fearful thoughts also filled my mind. How could God ever forgive my past life? How would I cope without my destructive, self-made support system? All I could do was muster up a tiny seed of hope that my life was not over.

When I entered my mother's house, I found my bedroom decorated with bright new bedding and cheery new curtains. My mum came in and sat down beside me. She was all hugs and smiles, ecstatic that her baby girl was home. I didn't realise it at the time, but God used the simple act of my mum sprucing up the bedroom to show me a glimpse of love and grace. And little did I know that the next few years would be filled with new friends, a college degree, a wedding and opportunities to mentor teenagers.

Looking back to that long drive home I would have never guessed that God would be so lavish in pouring out love on me, especially knowing it was nothing that I deserved or earned. God longs to lavish love on each of us. We can muster up a tiny seed of hope today that life is not over. With God, it is just beginning.

Prayer: *Dear God, take our tiny seeds of hope that you can change our lives, and show us your love and grace that awaits us. Amen*

Thought for the day: God has a parent's heart toward his children.

Natalie Guarascio (California, US)

Focus on Jesus

Read Philippians 4:4–9

Don't be anxious about anything; rather, bring up all of your requests to God in your prayers and petitions, along with giving thanks.
Philippians 4:6 (CEB)

For 14 years I worked in a sports shop in Anchorage, Alaska. One day as I was coming into the shop, an irate customer met me as I walked through the door. She was livid and began a tirade of complaints about a previous purchase. As I listened to her, I noticed that she had on a T-shirt with 'Focus on Jesus' written on the front. I thought to myself: 'You are one big hypocrite.' The Holy Spirit immediately brought me up short, saying, 'Are you going to lose your focus on Jesus, too?'

With a sigh, I admitted that my focus was more than a little blurry. I began to pray silently for the woman. Before I knew it, I felt God's peace and she regained her composure. She left as a satisfied customer, and I enjoyed God's peace in a way I never had before.

Philippians 4:6 comes to mind more and more as I seek to maintain my focus on Jesus: 'Don't be anxious about anything; rather, bring up all of your requests to God in your prayers and petitions, along with giving thanks.'

Prayer: *We thank you, dear God, for peace that you give in the midst of troubling moments. Help us call to you at such times so that we can be a channel of your love and understanding. Amen*

Thought for the day: Peace is only a prayer away.

Phil Cages (Alaska, US)

God Will!

Read Psalm 23:1–6
Even though I walk through the darkest valley, I fear no evil; for you are with me.
Psalm 23:4 (NRSV)

For many years the spirit of fear engulfed me. I feared almost everything—any situation and any undertaking. As a result, I endured many sleepless nights. Even when I slept, I would have strange nightmares. My fear was cast out on an ordinary day, while I was sitting in the front seat of a taxi.

The sticker on the dashboard read, 'My taxi is the best. Pay and rest. I will do the rest.' The sticker prompted me to ask myself, if I can rest in this taxi, how much more, can I rest in my Lord Jesus Christ? Isn't God the best? Can't I stop worrying, believe in God and rest? No sooner had I laid my fear before God than I felt a great sensation of relief. I found myself humming a song: 'Why do you worry, when you can pray? Trust in Jesus. He will be your guide.'

Faced with any difficult situation today, I say, 'Jesus is the best. I believe, trust in God and rest, and God will do the rest.'

Prayer: *Dear Lord Jesus, thank you for always being present with us in times of need. Amen*

Thought for the day: What fears can I leave in God's care today?

Duncan Charwadza (Harare, Zimbabwe)

Not too Late

Read Exodus 6:26—7:7

On the evening of that first day of the week… Jesus came and stood among them and said, 'Peace be with you!'… 'As the Father has sent me, I am sending you.'
John 20:19, 21 (NIV)

Three o'clock on a winter's afternoon. A hundred midges danced down a sunbeam as the day woke up—just for a while before it would be time to go to sleep again. Until then, overcast skies had imprisoned a morning mist but now a low watery sun glistened in a pastel sky, silhouetting tree shapes against dark foreboding mountains. Around me cattle raised their heads to scent the warming air, a blackbird chattered and I heard a cock crow—he was obviously confused about the time of day.

I have met people who feel that life's day has wakened too late for them. They have waited in vain for opportunities. They have known fulfilled, happy times but those have been shrouded in mists of care and uncertainty—the occasion for Christian service never seemed to come. But the day can often wake up late as it did for Moses and Aaron—called to God's special service in their 80s! Many like them can testify to their later years bringing opportunities to work for God.

Resurrection day must have been a long one for the disciples of Jesus—but when he came, late in the day, it was to commission them to new work. A lifetime may seem to have slipped by, but there is still work to do as long as the day lasts. The whole of life will have been a preparation for the evening glory.

Prayer: *Lord, take what is left of my day and make it radiant with your glory. Amen*

Thought for the day: It is never too late in the day to serve the Lord.

Colin Harbach (Cumbria, England)

Do Good Always

Read 1 Peter 3:8–17

Do not repay evil for evil or abuse for abuse; but, on the contrary, repay with a blessing. It is for this that you were called—that you might inherit a blessing.
1 Peter 3:9 (NRSV)

My sister Portia and her four children were ordered out of the house by her husband. He had decided to end their 20-year marriage. Our parents took her in, and soon we saw her slip into depression. A neighbour advised us to take her to a counsellor where my sister learned the importance of forgiveness. Then one day we noticed a great change; Portia was smiling.

She found a job and moved out of our parents' house. For the next ten years she brought up her children alone. The Lord guided her and the children. Later each one attended university.

Then one day Portia phoned to tell me that her ex-husband had died. Our family accompanied her to the funeral. A few months later she received word that her ex-husband's wife was dead. The couple left behind four children who were still at primary and secondary school. No one from the husband's family was willing to take the children, but Portia offered to do it. Her four working children helped her to take care of these orphans.

God worked miraculously. All eight children are now working, some overseas. Each one calls her 'mother'. Portia is a role model to me and to our community; she never repaid evil for evil. She is a testimony of what real love means.

Prayer: *O God, when we face rejection may your Holy Spirit help us to understand that forgiveness heals us. Amen*

Thought for the day: Even if the future appears bleak to us, God has another outlook.

Violet Mutasa (Mashonaland East, Zimbabwe)

Neighbours of Compassion

Read Luke 10:25–37

The lawyer asked Jesus, 'Who is my neighbour?'
Luke 10:29 (NRSV)

On 15 April 2013 two bombs exploded in Boston, Massachusetts, during the Boston Marathon. At least three people were killed and many others were severely injured.

As I listened later in the week to the latest news about this horrific event, I noticed that people from across the country began to show compassion for the victims, helping in whatever ways they could.

When a lawyer in today's reading approached Jesus, he asked which the greatest commandment was. Jesus asked the man what was written in the law. The lawyer answered correctly, but he questioned Jesus further: 'Who is my neighbour?'

Jesus then told him a parable about a good Samaritan. The one who showed compassion to the man injured by robbers proved to be the real neighbour—the same as those who showed compassion for the people in Boston, people they did not even know. They all showed the love which our Lord expects us to show for anyone in need. They were the true neighbours.

Prayer: *Dear Lord, today and every day show us who our neighbours are. May we see and respond to those who need your love expressed through our acts of compassion. Amen*

Thought for the day: Today I can show God's love to hurting people.

Roger Brannon (Florida, US)

Fatherhood

Read Matthew 1:18–24

Fathers, do not exasperate your children; instead, bring them up in the training and instruction of the Lord.

Ephesians 6:4 (NIV)

Watching the church youth group re-enact the nativity story, I developed a deeper appreciation for Joseph. As I viewed the scene where the angel of the Lord appeared to Joseph, instructing him to take Mary as his wife and name her son Jesus, I was struck by this thought: Jesus not only needed a mother, he needed an earthly father. I had always regarded Joseph as a minor influence in the birth and life of our Lord. Not so! God's infinite wisdom ordained that Joseph would serve as Jesus' earthly father. What a significant role and an awesome responsibility!

I volunteer in a Christian ministry that serves men who are homeless and addicted. Their past lives often reveal a common denominator: they were brought up in homes where their father was either absent or abusive. Their lives are in disarray, in part because their fathers failed them. One of the key aspects of the men's recovery teaches them the biblical principles of fatherhood. The objective is that those who have children will become the fathers that God intends them to be.

Every child deserves a godly father. If Jesus, God's Son, needed an earthly father to provide nurture and give guidance, how much more do we?

Prayer: *Compassionate God, we pray for fathers everywhere. Help them to see the importance of setting a godly example for their children to follow. Amen*

Thought for the day: Today I will give thanks for the godly father figures in my life.

Wayne W. Greenawalt (Illinois, US)

PRAYER FOCUS: CHILDREN OF ABUSIVE FATHERS

The Pause that Refreshes

Read Psalm 46:1–11

Be still, and know that I am God.
Psalm 46:10 (NIV)

Selah is a word used in the Bible, chiefly in the Psalms. While *selah* is a word of uncertain meaning, some have interpreted it to mean 'pause, and think of that'.

Pause? Even with my good intentions to study God's word daily, how often do I truly pause to ponder its truths? How often do I stop to 'smell the roses' in my life instead of focusing on the thorns? How often do I sincerely enjoy what God gives to me moment by moment?

Our lives can be extremely fast-paced, demanding and tiring. God recognises the need for us to refresh our souls and knows that such renewal can only be achieved if we slow down, take a deep breath and rest in his presence. That means setting aside all our distractions and turning our hearts and minds toward God.

Just as sleep is necessary for our physical health, pausing to reflect on God's goodness is required for our spiritual well-being. With God's help, I'll add *selah* to my daily practice.

Prayer: *Heavenly Father, please help us to pause and reflect on your goodness today. Amen*

Thought for the day: God is our true source of daily refreshment.

Kay L. Campbell (Connecticut, US)

A Super God

Read 1 Corinthians 12:27–31
God said, 'Let us make humankind in our image, according to our likeness.'
Genesis 1:26 (NRSV)

I was looking through some childhood mementoes—old photographs and the like—and I remembered how in my dreamy, idle moments as a youngster I would contemplate what I would do if I had certain superpowers like some of my comic-book heroes.

In reality, though, we all have superpowers: our skin can heal when it's been cut; broken bones can mend; we can see colour and movement, hear sounds, taste food, smell roses, recall happy memories. More importantly, we have the superpowers of patience, tolerance, understanding, empathy and love.

God has given us an astounding array of skills, functions and abilities—which all too often we take for granted. Just like those superheroes in the comics, we can put God's superpowers to great use with those around us every day, whether by offering physical or financial assistance, being willing to listen or by telling someone about the God who offers these gifts to all.

I may not be able to bend steel with my bare hands as I imagined in my childhood, but I hope that I can allow God's love to flow through me to all those I meet; to help the lost become found; to battle evil and injustice in the name of Jesus.

Prayer: *Source of strength, we thank you for the amazing powers you have given each of us through your Holy Spirit. Help us to use our gifts in ways that reflect your love and grace. Amen*

Thought for the day: How can my God-given powers benefit someone I encounter today?

John Porter (New South Wales, Australia)

Patience

Read Psalm 27:1–14

I remain confident of this: I will see the goodness of the Lord in the land of the living. Wait for the Lord; be strong and take heart and wait for the Lord.

Psalm 27:13–14 (NIV)

After struggling for months with breathing difficulties, my mother had a serious heart attack. Despite the care of many good doctors, the diagnosis and solution to her problems remain unclear. As an orthopaedic surgeon, I like to fix broken bones and to see immediate results; but I have learned to wait on the Lord for hope, perspective and healing.

Whether the problem is a broken bone or malfunctioning heart and lungs, we cannot always control the healing process; but the Lord is with us. Even without clear answers, I see the goodness of the Lord in the prayers and support of family members, colleagues and church members.

The most helpful doctors involved in my mother's care have taken the time to answer questions and to offer encouragement in hope and faith. They have inspired me to communicate confidence and the need to wait upon the Lord, regardless of the problem or the proposed solution.

Prayer: *Dear Lord, comfort those suffering from disease, especially when answers are not clear. Give them strength to be patient and to wait upon you for answers only you can give. Amen*

Thought for the day: Regardless of the problem, begin and end with faith.

Robert Boyce (Tennessee, US)

A Slug's Lesson

Read Matthew 5:13–16
Let your light shine before others, that they may see your good deeds and glorify your Father in heaven.
Matthew 5:16 (NIV)

I have always liked to observe the world around me, especially the tiny things. I remember one day I noticed marks on the wall that gleamed in the light. I realised that a slug had passed there. I did not need to see the slug because its tracks were there as evidence.

I began to reflect on this observation. I wondered if my spiritual life was as clear to others as the marks left by the slug. As Christians, we must leave marks of God's love in our journey. Our walk must reflect that Jesus is our Saviour, showing the love and mercy of Jesus Christ to those around us. What a wonderful lesson I learned by observing the tracks of this slug! Wherever we walk, we must leave the marks of Christians, saved by Jesus Christ.

Prayer: *O God, help us show those around us that we are Christians by sharing your love with the world. Amen*

Thought for the day: Does my daily life leave marks that point to Christ?

Carolina Maia Faria (Minas Gerais, Brazil)

That Distinct Voice

Read John 10:1–10

[The Shepherd] calls his own sheep by name and leads them out. When he has brought out all his own, he goes ahead of them, and the sheep follow him because they know his voice.

John 10:3–4 (NRSV)

Early in the morning, when my nephew Joe began to stir, I went to his crib, picked him up and carried him downstairs. My identical twin sister, Joe's mother, was cooking breakfast. 'Hi Joe,' she greeted him. He looked at her, looked back at me, and yelled, 'Mama!' as he held out both arms. My twin and I laughed as he distinguished his mother from the imposter.

Just as Joe recognised his mother's voice, we learn to recognise God's distinct voice. Sometimes, we hear his voice when we pray, when someone comes to mind or we feel the need to reach out to help or encourage. At other times, we hear God's voice in scripture. One verse might speak to our particular situation while another offers comfort, strength or peace.

We also hear God's voice through the Holy Spirit. John 16:13 (NRSV) says, 'When the Spirit of truth comes, he will guide you into all the truth; for he will not speak on his own, but will speak whatever he hears.' The Holy Spirit comforts, teaches and bears witness to the truth. The Spirit gives us discernment and wisdom to recognise God's voice and to walk with him.

Prayer: *Thank you, dear God, for reaching out to us and calling us to you. Help us to recognise the ways you speak to us. Amen*

Thought for the day: When we listen for God's voice, we will find comfort and truth.

Lin Daniels (Massachusetts, US)

Taming Fear

Read Genesis 50:15–21

We know that in all things God works for the good of those who love him, who have been called according to his purpose.
Romans 8:28 (NIV)

At the age of 60, and after 21 months of being in prison, I am preparing to be released. This causes me to think of the despair and fear I felt when I entered prison. I was angry and bitter. My wife divorced me. I lost everything I had. But God was revealed to me, and I began to learn what Job and Joseph learned: in times of tragedy, God does not leave us. In fact, God is never closer.

The stories of biblical heroes affirm the truth that when we are faced with opposition, faith restores us. God uses our trials to develop our character and faith. We naturally seek him most desperately when we are walking through life's valleys. I have learned that God is never closer than when I am in the valley. Fear strengthens faith and God awaits my earnest and sincere cry for help. He has used my time in prison to grow my faith and character beyond anything I thought possible. He stands ready to give us comfort and strength.

Prayer: *Dear God, sometimes we forget your promise to be with us and to sustain us. Forgive us, and help us to grow in faith. Amen*

Thought for the day: Our fears can bring us nearer to God.

W. Edward Clymer (Oklahoma, US)

Struggling to Pray

Read Matthew 6:9–15

Forgive us our debts, as we also have forgiven our debtors.
Matthew 6:12 (NIV)

I could not understand how someone I trusted could have committed such a horrible offence against me. That person had broken my trust so much that it seemed that everything I believed about the relationship was wrong. I was devastated and angry. Alone in my room, I tried to pray. 'Dear God,' I began, but I couldn't finish. The only thing I could do in my anguish was cry and moan.

I spoke with my sister-in-law, someone who has also been a spiritual sister to me, about my inability to pray. She suggested that I try praying the Lord's Prayer until I was able to put what was on my heart into words.

Even though it was difficult to do, I recited the prayer. When I got to 'Forgive us our debts, as we also have forgiven our debtors', I couldn't continue. I suddenly realised that I had done this very same thing to someone else years before. I wondered if that person had been as distraught as I had been in the past few days.

Too often I overlook the Lord's Prayer as something I say without really thinking about it. This experience helped me understand how important this prayer is, how important it is for me to forgive others and how much I need God's forgiveness.

Prayer: *Dear God, help us to remember the forgiveness you have shown us. Give us strength to offer that forgiveness to others as we pray, 'Father, hallowed be your name, your kingdom come. Give us each day our daily bread. Forgive us our sins, for we also forgive everyone who sins against us. And lead us not into temptation.'* Amen*

Thought for the day: We need to forgive as much as we need to be forgiven.

Sarah Negroni (Louisiana, US)

Speaking Forth God

Read John 20:30–31; 21:25

Let this be written for a future generation, that a people not yet created may praise the Lord.

Psalm 102:18 (NIV)

One of the joys of *The Upper Room* is being able to read the experiences of people worldwide and their encounters with God. We're united in our love of God and of the world he created and in sharing our thoughts together. I imagine people reading *The Upper Room* as they wake up each morning or go to bed at night, creating a continual outpouring of prayer and praise to God through the different time zones of the world.

When I consider that the psalmist's words are being read thousands of years after his death and think about the impact they have had on so many people, I wonder how what we produce might affect the next generation. All of us who love God and follow Jesus have something we can write about or speak about or sing about. Our words can help others to know and love God, too. We do it not for our own glory but for God's—for the sake of those not yet born.

The apostle John reckoned that the whole world couldn't hold the books that could be written to chronicle all that Jesus did while here on earth (see John 21:25). And Christ is still working in the world. Our stories and songs proclaim this good news every day.

Prayer: *We praise you, dear Lord, for all you do in our lives. May we show others your love and goodness so that they will praise you, too. Amen*

Thought for the day: How can I share of my faith with others today?

Pam Pointer (Wiltshire, England)

Strength and Weakness

Read 2 Corinthians 12:6–10

The Lord said to Paul, 'My grace is sufficient for you, for power is made perfect in weakness.'
2 Corinthians 12:9 (NRSV)

When I found out I had Type 1 diabetes, my life changed for ever. I was scared; but in time, I became more connected with my family, friends and God. I found out that when I'm weak, with God I can be strong.

Our pastor had asked my family to talk with the church about our experience with diabetes. I was nervous when the pastor asked us questions. I told him, 'I know that God will use my diabetes for good,' but I wasn't sure what the good would be.

I've had diabetes for three years now. I still get tired, and I get mad that I need to check my blood sugar seven or eight times a day and wear an insulin pump. But God has made me stronger; now I'm not as scared. Sometimes, I ask God why I have this disease and I hope that one day there will be a cure.

God has used my experience for good. After my family had spoken at our church, we heard about a man who had listened to the service. He had been diagnosed with diabetes and was struggling with all the changes he had to make. After he heard us, he thought, 'If that boy has the courage to deal with it, so have I.'

Everyone has something, and I have diabetes. With God's help, I'm going to do something good with it.

Prayer: *Thank you, dear God, for turning our weaknesses to strengths and for using our troubles for good. Amen*

Thought for the day: How does God give me strength in my weakness?

Chase Martin (Tennessee, US)

Small Group Questions

Wednesday 7 January

1. Have you ever struggled with your weight or your health? What was most difficult about that experience? How did the opinion of others affect your perception of your body either positively or negatively?

2. What changes have you made to your lifestyle in order to care for your body? Which changes were most difficult for you? Were the changes you made easy or difficult to maintain over time?

3. What spiritual practices do you use to support your lifestyle changes? How does reading scripture, praying or spending time with other Christians strengthen you and help you through these changes?

4. Besides eating, and reading scripture, in what other areas do you struggle to find the right balance in 'diet'? How does this meditation apply to those areas?

5. How does your community of faith encourage healthy living? What are some other ways your congregation could support people who are struggling either physically or spiritually?

6. What ways have you discovered to motivate yourself to read the Bible and pray more often?

Wednesday 14 January

1. Think about a difficult person in your life. What traits or habits do you find most annoying or challenging to deal with? How do you feel when you meet this person? How do you usually act toward him or her?

2. Danielle challenges us to speak blessings on the difficult people in our lives. What blessings do these people bring to your life? What do you admire about them? What compliment or word of encouragement might you offer the next time you meet?

3. Think about someone who seems to share God's love easily with the people they encounter. What traits or habits do you admire in this person? What can you learn from their actions? What new practice can you adopt to help you share God's love and compassion with the world?

4. How do you pray for difficult people in your life? What do you ask for on their behalf? What do you pray for yourself and your relationships with difficult people?

5. How does your church community share God's love with the world? What practices in your congregation remind or encourage members to treat all people with love and respect? Are there ways your church could work harder to bless others? In what ways does it also vilify others at times?

Wednesday 21 January

1. How do you feel about sharing your faith in public? Does reading your Bible in a public setting make you feel self-conscious? Do you enjoy talking to strangers about your faith?

2. What is your first memory of talking about your faith with a stranger or non-family member? Describe that experience. How did that experience affect how you share your faith today?

3. Do you think that the Bible is advocating one approach to sharing faith for all of us? How have you experienced others sharing their faith with you? Did it happen mostly through words? Actions? Presence?

4. If you could tell a non-believer one story of how God has been present in your life, what would you talk about? Why would you choose this story?

5. When have you felt that you needed to hide your faith? Where were you? Who was present? Why did you want to hide your faith? What did you do?

6. How does your church encourage you to share your faith? What study groups or practices encourage members to share their faith with others?

7. In what other areas are we tempted to become friends of the world?

Wednesday 28 January

1. What is your first memory of grief? Who was the first loved one you lost? What emotions do you recall from these experiences?

2. Which individuals or communities have you turned to for support during times of grief? How did they help? What did these people do or say that was particularly helpful or comforting? How did they make it harder?

3. Do you have experience of supporting others in times of grief? Is that easy or difficult for you? What do you do to be supportive?

4. How have experiences of death and grief changed your relationship with God? Did grief draw you closer to God and strengthen your faith or did it cause you to doubt God or your faith?

5. Do you agree with Anthony when he writes, 'Every trial can bring us closer to God—if we let it.' Why or why not?

6. What Bible passages do you turn to in times of grief or distress? Describe how these scriptures give you comfort, encouragement, or models for dealing with difficult experiences.

Wednesday 4 February

1. Recall a time when you struggled to believe or trust God. Describe how you felt. What questions did you have about your faith or about God? Did you express your doubts to anyone? If so, to whom?

2. How have you observed other Christians responding when you or someone expresses doubts? Were these responses helpful or not? Why?

3. What does your church community or pastor tell you about having doubts about faith or about God? In your experience, is expressing doubt acceptable in your church? What happens when someone admits doubt in your congregation?

4. Gale writes: 'The remedy for doubt is trust and prayer.' Do you agree or disagree with this statement? If you agree, describe how trust and prayer can remedy doubt. What prayer practices have helped you to overcome doubt?

5. Not all of our doubts are directed toward God or faith. What other areas do you find are the focus of your doubt? Are these areas somehow inter-related? Do you think doubt is a personality trait that is present more or less in individuals? Is the opposite of doubt faith, or certainty, or confidence, or something else?

Wednesday 11 February

1. Recall a time when you didn't know how or what to pray. What did you do? Did you tell God that you didn't know what to pray? Did you ask him to help you know what to pray? Did you pray a simple, general prayer? Did you decide not to pray at that moment?

2. Apart from when someone is nearing death, what other situations do you think make it difficult to know what to pray for? Have you shared your uncertainty about what to pray with others? What advice have you received?

3. How does your church handle these situations in the time of prayer during worship? Do you think the approach is helpful? Does your church talk openly about sometimes not knowing how to pray?

4. Cathy turned to words from the Lord's Prayer when she was not sure how to pray. Do you do that too? What other prayers, passages or words do you turn to when you are not sure how to pray?

5. Do you think the effectiveness of your prayers is dependent on your words? Do you think the words are most helpful for you, for God, or for the one for whom you pray? How do you think one might go about expanding the language one has available for prayer? Romans 8:26 tells us that 'The Spirit helps us in our weakness. We do not know what we ought to pray for, but the Spirit… intercedes for us with groans that words cannot express.' How does this passage relate to today's topic?

Wednesday 18 February

1. How does your church observe Lent? What practices, if any, are suggested for members of the congregation during this season?

2. What Lenten practices have you observed? Do you do the same thing each year? What benefits have you experienced from these practices? What challenges?

3. What did you think of Edward's approach to Lent—changing it from a season of giving up something to a season of looking for new ways to give? Do you think this is a practice you might want to try? How do you think it might change your experience of the season of Lent?

4. What opportunities are you aware of in your community to reach out to those 'without'?

5. What does your church do to reach out to those who are suffering or in need, especially during the season of Lent? How might you get involved? What do you feel called to do?

Wednesday 25 February

1. What were you taught about 'keeping the Sabbath' as you were growing up? Were there specific rules about what you should do and what you should not do? Have those rules changed for you over your lifetime? What personal guidelines do you have for keeping the Sabbath today?

2. What do you think of the lesson Matthew's father taught him? Do you agree that what his father proposed was an opportunity to 'worship God in a different way'? Do you think this was a good way to keep the Sabbath?

3. What does your church teach about the Sabbath? Are there particular ways in which you are invited to keep the Sabbath? Is Sunday worship only a part of that, or are there other opportunities/suggestions as well?

4. Do you think it is important to have some 'Sabbath time' every day, or at least on a regular basis? What does Sabbath mean to you? Rest? Focus on God? Something different from the ordinary routine of days?

5. Why do you think Sabbath is part of the Christian tradition? What is its purpose? Is it primarily designed for God's sake or for our sake? How do you think our culture supports or undermines the idea of Sabbath?

Wednesday 4 March

1. How do you observe Lent? Do you give something up? Do you begin a new practice? If you have never observed Lent in this way, why do you think others find these practices important?

2. What have you learned about God and yourself through denying yourself something you enjoy?

3. What do you think of Janet's Lenten practice? Is it one that you might consider taking up? Why or why not?

4. Besides making time for Bible study, what are some positive practices we might take up for Lent? Which would you be most likely to adopt and why?

5. How might taking up a positive practice or denying yourself something you enjoy help you to identify more closely with Jesus as Easter approaches?

6. What spiritual practices help you to feel closer to Christ?

Wednesday 11 March

1. Bonnie describes a scar that bore witness to a person's faith. When have you seen or become aware of a scar, either physical or emotional, that revealed something about someone's faith?

2. What scars do you have on your body? Can you remember how you got them? What story do your scars tell about you and your life?

3. Isaiah 53:5 states, 'By his wounds we are healed.' What does this statement mean to you? Is it important to you that Jesus suffered and died? Why or why not?

4. Our hurts and scars can make us more empathetic to the suffering of others. How has this been true in your own life? How have you been able to care for others better because of your own hurtful experiences?

5. How does your church offer healing to those who suffer? What ministries and resources are available for those in need? How can you support these ministries and show God's love to others?

Wednesday 18 March

1. Describe your worst experience with a community of faith. How did this experience affect your personal relationship with God? How have you begun to heal from this experience? Who has helped you to heal?

2. Describe your best experience with a community of faith. What made this experience positive? How has this positive experience shaped your faith? How have your experiences both positive and negative changed the way you mix with new members of your community?

3. Karline writes, 'Each of us needs to belong to a community of faith.' Do you agree or disagree with this statement. Why?

4. What does it mean to you to be 'grafted into God's family'? How would you describe this experience to others?

5. What evidence does your church give the community around you that you are followers of Christ? How do you display the fruit of the Spirit in your worship and outreach?

Wednesday 25 March

1. Have you ever complained to God? Is this a common part of your prayer life? If so, why? If not, what do your prayers usually include?

2. Peggy writes in this meditation that she expected God to be displeased. When have you worried that God might be displeased with you? Why did you expect God's displeasure? What did you do in light of this expectation?

3. When have you felt that God was pleased with you? How did you know? What action or prayer led to this feeling? How did you respond?

4. What do you think of when you hear the word 'offering'? What are some different kinds of offerings you might give to God? Which of these offerings is the easiest for you to give? Which are most difficult?

Wednesday 1 April

1. What is your experience with cancer? Have you or has someone you love been diagnosed with cancer? How did that diagnosis affect you?

2. What prayers, spiritual practices or scripture passages help you in times of fear and illness?

3. When you or a loved one face serious illness, does your faith provide comfort? How so? If not, how has your faith been negatively affected by experiences with serious illness?

4. Kathleen writes that relationship with Jesus and assurance of salvation changed her perspective. How does Jesus' death and resurrection 'change everything' for you?

5. Recall a time when you found it difficult to trust God. What made trusting hard at that time? Who or what helped you to regain confidence in God? What encouragement would you offer to someone who struggles to trust God?

Wednesday 8 April

1. Think of someone you really enjoy talking with. What are some common topics of conversation? What makes conversations with this person particularly enjoyable?

2. Do you ever gossip? How does it feel to gossip with a good friend? Have you ever been in a situation where you regretted gossiping? What happened? Did this experience cause you to change your behaviour?

3. Have you ever been the subject of someone else's gossiping? How did it feel to be gossiped about? How did you respond?

4. What do you think of Deanna's practice of 'Stop, breathe and pray' as a way of curbing gossip and unkind words? Is this a practice that might be helpful to you? In what other areas of your life might you apply this practice?

Wednesday 15 April

1. Natalie describes a time when she made a drastic change. When have you made a drastic change in your life? What did that feel like? What pushed you to make that change? How did others respond to your decision?

2. When you are fearful, what do you do? Where do you turn for reassurance? What prayers, Bible verses or songs help to comfort you and give you confidence?

3. Describe a time when people went out of their way to make you feel welcome. What did they do? How did you respond to their gestures of hospitality?

4. How do you make others feel welcome and loved? Who in your life needs your love and care just now? How might you show God's love to him or her?

5. Where in your church or community do you see God's love being demonstrated? Who is participating? Who is being helped? How might you join in?

Wednesday 22 April

1. Was *selah* a familiar word for you? If so, how had you heard it described or defined?

2. Read Psalm 46, paying attention to the word *selah* when it appears. How is your experience of reading the psalm different after reading Kay's meditation?

3. What helps you remember to pause and rest during your day? What practices have you heard others using to help them take time for prayer or rest on a regular basis? What new practice might you adopt to encourage you to pause even when you are busy?

4. Describe a time when you noticed and took time to savour God's blessings in your life. Who or what helped you to do this? How did you respond to the blessing you had been given?

5. How does your church encourage you to make time for God in your daily life? What prayer groups, Bible studies or other structured events help you carve out time for your faith during the week?

Wednesday 29 April

1. What do you enjoy most about *The Upper Room*? How do you use these meditations in your daily spiritual practice? How might you share this practice with others in your community?

2. How does being connected to people around the world through this magazine shape your prayer life? What blessings and challenges come from being part of a worldwide Christian community?

3. Pam writes that 'our words can help others to know and love God'. How do you help others know and love God? With words? With actions?

4. Think about the person who has been most influential in your faith journey. How has that person helped you grow in faith? What have they done or said to demonstrate God's love to you?

5. How does your church teach younger generations about the Christian faith? How are older generations passing along wisdom to young people? In what other ways could your church help young people to grow in faith?

Journal page

Journal page

Journal page

Reflecting the Glory

Bible readings and reflections for Lent and Easter

Tom Wright

'You can't love an abstraction. You can't even love the idea of love. You can only truly love a person. The deepest, richest meaning of love must be personal love. The relevance of knowing God in Jesus is that when we love God in Jesus we discover how that love, that personal love, is given to us in order that it may be given through us.'

This book of Bible readings and reflections, for every day from Ash Wednesday to the first Sunday of Easter, explores how we reveal Jesus even at the lowest and weakest points of our lives. Drawing on New Testament passages, with a particular focus on Paul's letters to the church in Corinth, Tom Wright shows that through God's Holy Spirit, the suffering but also the glory of Christ can be incarnate in our lives, enabling us to be the people of God for the world.

ISBN 978 0 7459 3556 0   £8.99

To order a copy of this book, please turn to the order form on page 159.

Using the Jesus Prayer

Steps to a simpler Christian life

John Twisleton

In a hectic world, we so often struggle to find ways of growing in faith and, especially, deepening our experience of prayer. While many have been inspired by documentaries about contemplative prayer and monastic life, it remains a challenge to sustain disciplines of prayer and worship in the busyness of everyday life.

The Jesus Prayer of Eastern Orthodoxy, 'Lord Jesus Christ, Son of God, have mercy on me, a sinner', offers a simple yet profound way of developing such discipline. Thoroughly biblical, carried forward by the faith of the Church through the centuries, it stands as a unique gift and a task for us. In this book on the Jesus Prayer, its succinct summary of faith and its capacity to empower, John Twisleton gives practical guidance on how to use it, as well as exploring the simplicity of life it offers.

ISBN 978 1 84101 778 5   £6.99

To order a copy of this book, please turn to the order form on page 159.

Living Liturgies

Transition time resources for services, prayer and conversation with older people

Caroline George

This book offers a creative worship resource for pastoral ministry with those at an often overlooked time of life—the move from independent living to dependency, or from the 'third age' to the 'fourth age' of life. The twelve liturgies—and accompanying reflections for those leading the worship—were developed by Caroline George after many years of working in church and community settings with older people and provide valuable help for those embarking on this ministry, as well as inspiration for those already involved.

Each specially written liturgy uses a simple structure based around a theme to weave together experience, scripture and the assurance of God's love and grace. Conversation is used to connect the theme with past, present and future, leading into prayer and silent reflection with the help of a visual aid.

ISBN 978 0 85746 323 4   £7.99
To order a copy of this book, please turn to the order form on page 159.

Deep Calls to Deep

Spiritual formation in the hard places of life

Tony Horsfall

The Psalms offer honest insights into the reality of life with God, reflecting every human emotion and situation. Through looking at some of the Psalms written 'from the depths', we can understand more fully the way in which God is at work to shape our characters and form the life of Christ within us during difficult times. This book offers reflections drawn from selected Psalms to guide us as we begin to make sense of our own history with God, and also point us to how we can get to know God better here and now, preparing us for whatever may lie ahead.

Deep Calls to Deep will speak to those who are 'passing through the valley' but it will also be of help to anyone who desires a deeper walk with God, as well as those who accompany others on their Christian journey, as mentors, soul friends or spiritual directors.

ISBN 978 1 84101 731 0   £7.99
To order a copy of this book, please turn to the order form on page 159.

How to encourage Bible reading in your church

BRF has been helping individuals connect with the Bible for over 90 years. We want to support churches as they seek to encourage church members into regular Bible reading.

Order a Bible reading resources pack

This pack is designed to give your church the tools to publicise our Bible reading notes. It includes:

- Sample Bible reading notes for your congregation to try.
- Publicity resources, including a poster.
- A church magazine feature about Bible reading notes.

The pack is free, but we welcome a £5 donation to cover the cost of postage. If you require a pack to be sent outside the UK or require a specific number of sample Bible reading notes, please contact us for postage costs. More information about what the current pack contains is available on our website.

How to order and find out more

- Visit www.biblereadingnotes.org.uk/for-churches/
- Telephone BRF on 01865 319700 between 9.15 am and 5.30 pm.
- Write to us at BRF, 15 The Chambers, Vineyard, Abingdon, OX14 3FE.

Keep informed about our latest initiatives

We are continuing to develop resources to help churches encourage people into regular Bible reading, wherever they are on their journey. Join our email list at **www.biblereadingnotes.org.uk/helpingchurches/** to stay informed about the latest initiatives that your church could benefit from.

Introduce a friend to our notes

We can send information about our notes and current prices for you to pass on. Please contact us.

Subscriptions

The Upper Room is published in January, May and September.

Individual subscriptions

The subscription rate for orders for 4 or fewer copies includes postage and packing: THE UPPER ROOM annual individual subscription   £16.20

Church subscriptions

Orders for 5 copies or more, sent to ONE address, are post free:
THE UPPER ROOM annual church subscription   £12.75

Please do not send payment with order for a church subscription. We will send an invoice with your first order.

Please note that the annual billing period for church subscriptions runs from 1 May to 30 April.

Copies of the notes may also be obtained from Christian bookshops.

Single copies of *The Upper Room* will cost £4.25. Prices valid until 30 April 2016.

Giant print version

The Upper Room is available in giant print for the visually impaired, from:

Torch Trust for the Blind
Torch House
Torch Way,
Northampton Road
Market Harborough
LE16 9HL

Tel: 01858 438260
www.torchtrust.org

Individual Subscriptions

☐ I would like to take out a subscription myself (complete your name and address details only once)

☐ I would like to give a gift subscription (please complete both name and address sections below)

Your name...

Your address...

....Postcode..

Your telephone number...

Gift subscription name...

Gift subscription address..

....Postcode..

Gift message (20 words max)...

....

Please send *The Upper Room* beginning with the May 2015 / September 2015 / January 2016 issue: (delete as applicable)

THE UPPER ROOM ☐ £16.20

Please complete the payment details below and send, with appropriate payment, to: BRF, 15 The Chambers, Vineyard, Abingdon OX14 3FE

Total enclosed £ .... (cheques should be made payable to 'BRF')

Payment by ☐ cheque ☐ postal order ☐ Visa ☐ Mastercard ☐ Switch

Card no:																		

Expires: ☐☐☐☐   Security code: ☐☐☐

Issue no (Switch): ☐☐☐☐

Signature (essential if paying by credit/Switch card) ....

☐ Please do not send me further information about BRF publications

☐ Please send me a Bible reading resources pack to encourage Bible reading in my church

BRF is a Registered Charity

Church Subscriptions

☐ Please send me ... copies of *The Upper Room* May 2015 / September 2015 / January 2016 issue (delete as applicable)

Name...

Address ....

....Postcode...................................

Telephone ....

Email..

Please send this completed form to:
BRF, 15 The Chambers, Vineyard, Abingdon OX14 3FE

Please do not send payment with this order. We will send an invoice with your first order.

Christian bookshops: All good Christian bookshops stock BRF publications. For your nearest stockist, please contact BRF.

Telephone: The BRF office is open between 09.15 and 17.30. To place your order, telephone 01865 319700; fax 01865 319701.

Web: Visit www.brf.org.uk

☐ Please send me a Bible reading resources pack to encourage Bible reading in my church

BRF is a Registered Charity

ORDERFORM

REF	TITLE	PRICE	QTY	TOTAL
3556 0	Reflecting the Glory	£8.99		
778 5	Using the Jesus Prayer	£6.99		
323 4	Living Liturgies	£7.99		
731 0	Deep Calls to Deep	£7.99		

POSTAGE AND PACKING CHARGES						
Order value	UK	Europe	Surface	Air Mail		
Under £7.00	£1.25	£3.00	£3.50	£5.50		
£7.00–£29.99	£2.25	£5.50	£6.50	£10.00		
£30.00 and over	FREE	prices on request				

Postage and packing	
Donation	
TOTAL	

Name _____ Account Number _____

Address _____

_____ Postcode _____

Telephone Number_____

Email _____

Payment by: ❏ Cheque ❏ Mastercard ❏ Visa ❏ Postal Order ❏ Maestro

Card no ❏❏❏❏ ❏❏❏❏ ❏❏❏❏ ❏❏❏❏ ❏❏❏

Valid from ❏❏❏❏   Expires ❏❏❏❏   Issue no. ❏❏❏

Security code* ❏❏❏   *Last 3 digits on the reverse of the card.
ESSENTIAL IN ORDER TO PROCESS YOUR ORDER   Shaded boxes for Maestro use only

Signature _____ Date _____

All orders must be accompanied by the appropriate payment.

Please send your completed order form to:
BRF, 15 The Chambers, Vineyard, Abingdon OX14 3FE
Tel. 01865 319700 / Fax. 01865 319701 Email: enquiries@brf.org.uk

❏ Please send me further information about BRF publications.

Available from your local Christian bookshop.   BRF is a Registered Charity